THE NEW CORPORATE CITIZEN

THE NEW CORPORATE CITIZEN

AN INNOVATIVE MODEL OF CORPORATE PHILANTHROPY

If you're reading this book you're the right person for the job! ~ Cara Nichols

CARA NICHOLS

Hardcover ISBN: 978-1-5445-2719-2
Paperback ISBN: 978-1-5445-0421-6
eBook ISBN: 978-1-5445-0420-9

"Do what you can, with what you have, where you are."
—Theodore Roosevelt

"Rackspace is the only major corporation in our area,
and as a result, we've really become part of the neighborhood.
Some people say we're creating a new model, and maybe we
are. But what we're really deciding to do is be part of our
neighborhood, be a citizen of our part of town. And to make a
difference here. To make it better."
—Graham Weston

This book is dedicated to all the underdogs,
and to the underdog in each of us.

CONTENTS

FOREWORD

BY GRAHAM WESTON

This is not a book about the inner workings of a managed cloud company, an early internet service pioneer, or a startup that celebrated $1.5 million in annual sales in its early years only to quickly grow into a multibillion-dollar enterprise employing thousands around the world.

This is a book about creating community, about leveraging success at Rackspace as a tech company to make a difference in the lives of our neighbors. It's a book about how service to our customers, which we branded "Fanatical Support" then and which has now evolved to "Fanatical Experience™," was transformed to reach out and connect with the people around our corporate headquarters. It's a book about how you, too, can take the model we created and apply it to your own company and community.

If there is a single lesson that Rackspace executives learned from our community investment, it is this: We had a duty to do our best each day to provide the best possible service to our customers, and an equal obligation to share the fruits of that success. Our neighbors, we decided, were a distinct class of shareholders, and we became determined to deliver them a positive return. They knew we wanted them to benefit from our success.

What they might not have known is that they were giving us the opportunity to become a better company and better human beings in the process.

And this is where the topic of this book—becoming true contributors—really began. At this point in Rackspace's history, we were established. We had become grown-ups, developed our own unique culture, and realized that even though our work was based in technology, we were effectively a service company.

To accommodate our growth, we had just moved our headquarters to a vacant shopping mall on the economically depressed northeast side of San Antonio. We got a sense of the neighborhood pretty quickly: the nearby public schools were uniformly underfunded, largely invisible to the distant business community, and working-class families whose children attended the schools had no means of their own to elevate public education outcomes. Rackspace was the only corporate citizen on the block, metaphorically speaking. But more than that, we wanted it to be clear that we were committed to being more than just tenants who shared the same zip code.

So what exactly did we do? Right from the start, we decided to "adopt" seven schools that were in our immediate vicinity. There was no playbook that existed for companies adopting schools, so we went in and talked to students, teachers, and administrative staff about their needs, learning as we went. We made mistakes along the way, but we adjusted our path when we needed to and learned to focus our efforts. We became excellent listeners and enablers.

That our efforts succeeded is becoming more and more apparent—many of the kids from those early days who enrolled in the tech magnet program and our one-on-one workplace mentorship program are now working at Rackspace in responsible, well-paid positions. This small community around Rackspace takes great pride in the company's accomplishments. Rackspace is part of them.

The positive return to our business of investing in the neighborhood played an invaluable role in creating a strong, identifiable reputation for Rackspace among people who may have considered us just another company. Today, even if people do not always know what Rackspace does, they know that we are engaged in their community, that we care, and they understand our values.

As a result of this approach—investing in your own backyard, some call it—I have become deeply committed to the belief that businesses have a role to play by stepping in and filling the gap that always exists between government services and true need. There is a confluence between federal and state programs and the point at which private citizens see the opportunity for improvements that are freer of regulation and intensely responsive to local needs. This begins by businesses recognizing that they are not only products of, but in service to, the communities they come from.

The New Corporate Citizen is your business's guide to becoming a true contributor to your community in a profoundly authentic and intimate way. It is the playbook we wish we had all those years ago. And it is told from the perspective of the person who led those efforts by diving deeply into relationships, building trust, and, perhaps most importantly, investing our employees in the future of this community. Cara Nichols did not have a formal pedigree in community affairs, but what she did have—and still does—is a heart for the work and a willingness to figure it out. And along the way, a new model emerged that we are proud to share with you.

I believe a company's commitment can pull communities together and produce unexpected and inspiring results. How Rackspace got there—through trial and error, I will admit—is less important than the fact that we hope other businesses and their leaders will use and refine this model for the benefit of their own communities and enjoy the very visible rewards that flow back in return. If and when they do, there is truly very little that could make me feel more of a contributor.

INTRODUCTION

Allie looked out into the faces of the second graders gathered around her and asked a simple question.

"Does anyone know what Rackspace does?" she asked, referring to the tech company turned philanthropic giant for seven schools in a socioeconomically disadvantaged San Antonio neighborhood. Allie, along with many other Rackers wearing their signature school-bus-yellow volunteer T-shirts, was in one of those schools that morning—Camelot Elementary, on the city's northeast side.

One little girl's hand shot up, and her answer was everything.

"You help people!" she answered, a little shy at having been called on.

Allie smiled. The little girl was right.

Besides helping customers with their IT solutions, Rackspace, through the Rackspace Foundation, is dedicated to helping schools in the community. It struck Allie—and me, later, when she recounted the story—that children recognized our work in their schools. Those yellow T-shirts weren't just bright and colorful; they were hopeful. And kids were noticing.

A VISION, A REALITY

The Rackspace Foundation currently sponsors seven schools (the "Magnificent Seven") and the neighborhoods that surround them. The schools—four elementary schools, two middle schools, and one high school—are Title I schools, meaning they have a large percentage of economically disadvantaged children and receive federal funding to help ensure students' success. In some of those schools, as many as 100 percent of the kids are on the free or reduced-price lunch program. A significant number of the kids are English-language learners. All seven schools are within about 2.5 miles of the Rackspace headquarters and, in total, serve almost 7,500 kids.

Because of the volume of kids and their proximity to Rackspace's office, they're very much on the radar of Rackspace employees. When Rackers come to work in the morning, they drive through the neighborhoods that house the kids they help. Walking through the parking lot into the office, the marching band can be heard next door at the high school they sponsor. In total, the Rackspace Foundation has invested over $6 million in initiatives and programs that improve the lives of students, all in its own backyard—school beautification projects, enhanced Teacher Appreciation Weeks, holiday food drives...the list goes on and on. In the Rackspace Foundation, the schools have an ally. A partner. A support system.

Such progress would not be possible without the support of Rackspace (the corporate entity, separate from the foundation), and Rackers themselves, who donate to the foundation and volunteer in its adopted schools. What is Rackspace, you ask? Let's take a quick look.

THE "FANATICAL EXPERIENCE™" PROMISE

Rackspace itself is a company that delivers IT-as-a-service to mid- and enterprise-sized customers across a variety of industries and locations around the world, in both the private and public sectors. In everything Rackspace does, the tagline is "Fanatical Experience™," ensuring customers have a seamless, delightful experience with the company.

The vein of support that runs through Rackspace as a business also informs its charitable endeavors. For example, in a program called Rack Gives Back, Rackspace gives a portion of its corporate revenue to nonprofits that primarily serve STEAM—science, tech, engineering, arts, and math—initiatives for the K–12 population. The Rackspace Foundation itself is funded by individual current Rackers through voluntary payroll deductions, as well as others who believe in the mission of supporting neighborhood schools.

Rackspace would not be a $2 billion company if not for one of the founders and my personal hero, Graham Weston. A powerhouse entrepreneur, he took a teeny San Antonio-based startup and invested his time, money, and talent to help—along with many others—turn the company into what it is today, a global enterprise. Graham is a visionary leader, and even when he was chairman of such a large company (Rackspace's office is literally a renovated shopping mall), he knew Rackers by name. More important than that, though, is his generosity. He is the heart behind so much of not only the business's progress but also its community endeavors and philanthropic efforts.

Graham believes in Rackspace, and he believed in me when I joined the company in 2009. Throughout my ten years of service, I led the global Community Affairs programs for Rackspace and served as the President of the Board of the Rackspace Foundation. When I became a Racker, the foundation was just getting off the ground. When I left, it was a self-sustaining, employee-funded fixture in the community. And although I'm incredibly proud to have accomplished all that you'll read about in this story, by no means was there a playbook for what we did or how we did it. And besides the start of my career when I briefly taught third and fourth grade, I definitely didn't have the pedigree to do what we did. But step by step, and with the help of many, the Rackspace Foundation became the stake in the ground, the signal to the community that they had an advocate.

I grew up in San Antonio, went to college at the University of Texas at Austin, and made my way to New York after graduating. In an in-between time in my life, I decided to get my teaching certificate until I could decide what I really wanted to do when I grew up. I found my way back to Texas, and after those four years of teaching and a side hustle writing, I helped start a local lifestyle and culture magazine. In 2008, when the economy tanked, so did my publication. I reached out to Rackspace's chief strategy officer at the time, Lew Moorman, whom I'd connected with in my editor days, and he offered me a contract position as a copywriter and blogger focused on the cloud. At the time, I didn't even know what cloud technology was, but I went with it. Then I started coming into the office—and I never left.

A few months later, I was offered a full-time job at Rackspace, eventually leading copywriters and designers, but I always had my eye on the prize: leading Community Affairs and getting to work on the Rackspace Foundation. When it became available, I knew I had to go for it; I knew what it was like to be a teacher, have always been socially minded, and knew I wanted to give back to teachers, the kids they served, and their communities. The Rackspace Foundation and Graham gave me that opportunity.

A NEW WAY TO GIVE BACK

When the Rackspace Foundation was first launched, it was more or less a loose idea of how to plug into the community. The creators of the foundation knew what they wanted it to be—a mechanism of community support through education—but were open to how they might get there. They decided to holistically support local schools—a discovery process I'll explain later in this book—and realized along the way they were breaking new ground.

We continued that mission by creating and evolving a new model that businesses can use to help schools. Our model involves both the company and the foundation it created and supports strategic school-time activities (like bolstering classrooms with technology or teaching age-appropriate financial literacy courses), as well as outside enrichment programs (like hosting summer camps and sponsoring chess programs). There is so much more that the foundation does, and I can't wait to share it with you in this book.

For now, though, I want to explain what this book is and why it matters to you. As a leader in your business, if you're reading this, you likely are already investing in your community in some way or are considering the best way to do so. Perhaps your company partners with United Way for its philanthropic endeavors or follows the charitable lead of the CEO or other civically involved business leader. Or perhaps your organization takes what I call the "peanut butter spread" approach, which is to give a little bit of funding to every nonprofit, to whichever cause feels right in the moment—or, frankly, to whoever asks. In any of these scenarios, giving portfolios can be as varied as the number of nonprofits in any given city and can include anything from cancer research to literacy to STEAM to sponsoring 5K runs and golf tournaments. Although that approach can feel good and even sounds good on the surface, it's hard to dial in support and see your direct impact on those in your backyard when your funds are so spread across the board.

I want to be clear: all giving is valuable. Even "peanut butter spread" activities, in which you spread your donations around, can be helpful and likely won't cause any harm. However, I am sharing this method with you now because I believe we found a more efficient way to allocate resources and funds to make a difference, and that difference starts with neighborhood schools. In our experience, especially if you have a community in your neighborhood entrenched in generational poverty, these types of holistic programs will give students a lens to see outside of their circumstances. Who knows, maybe one day they'll even come work for your company. It happens at Rackspace all the time!

In this book, I will teach you the Rackspace Foundation method that is:

- **Flexible.** Schools do receive federal and state funds, but they're steeped in rigid requirements and may not be able to address the true needs of the students. In our model, schools are invited to have a voice in addressing what they feel their students need and have the autonomy to put donated dollars to best use. And programs can flex with the changing needs of schools, teachers, grade levels, and students. As a corporate funder, you can ensure the causes you support target real needs and reflect your real company values.

- **Scalable.** The Rackspace Foundation has worked with seven schools from the start, but our method is and always has been scalable. The beauty of being a corporate funder is that you can start as small or large as you feel comfortable with. You don't even have to start with an entire school. Start with one classroom. Pull back if you need to and grow when you can.

- **Accessible.** I don't have a background in nonprofit management or social entrepreneurism. I have learned over the past decade, though, of something more important: the value of being an empathetic listener and of caring for the well-being of those you serve—not only your customers but the broader community as well. If this feels new and scary to you, that's okay. The head part will come. The heart part is what's required right now. If you're still with me, you have it.

- **Strategic.** In your business, you're accustomed to a certain ability to change the rules of engagement to some degree to suit the conditions of the market. You can adapt to better meet the needs of your customers or shareholders. The education system, however, is not set up to move as quickly. You have an opportunity to help schools get the best return on your investment—a move that will ultimately support your true stakeholders, the children.

- **Responsive.** Often, we find educators know what their students need, but they don't have all the abilities or resources their students require to succeed. Although a teacher's job description may simply be to educate students, in reality they also serve as counselor, cheerleader, tutor, writer, nurse, volunteer, firefighter and police officer (not literally), motivator, parent liaison, and IT help desk staff. But by and large, what educators *don't* do is turn away. They have one of the most important jobs in the world, and they don't get to cherry-pick their students. Oftentimes, their students' lives can be messy, and try as they might, they can't always just leave their problems at the door. If you leverage bits and pieces of our model, you can respond to those true needs and empower teachers to be all that they are truly required to be.

- **Beneficial to the company.** The Rackspace Foundation gives Rackers the feeling of unity and inspiration—a sense of higher purpose. When you know that you're doing meaningful work and that you're a part of something bigger than yourself, you try harder. You show up a little more. You engage more deeply with colleagues and the causes (or, in our case, schools and kids) you're rallying around. The passion you get from helping is contagious— the good kind of contagious. The Rackspace Foundation has served Rackspace well, and this model will help inspire your employees and create similar returns for your organization.

In the following pages, you'll find an explanation of our method, including stories about our particular experience—and, more importantly, insight and inspiration for how you can leverage elements of it in your own business. That practical advice comes in Part II of this book. Before we can get there, though, you need to better understand who Rackspace and the Rackspace Foundation are and what they do.

PART I

THE RACKSPACE FOUNDATION
AND THE MAGNIFICENT SEVEN

CHAPTER 1

MAKING A COMMITMENT
THE FIRST TWO YEARS

In 2005, Hurricane Katrina displaced over one million people. When then-mayor of San Antonio Phil Hardberger announced the city would shelter many of the victims, Graham Weston, real estate investor and Rackspace's chairman at the time, took action. He had property—an old building that previously housed a Montgomery Ward and was connected to the former Windsor Park Mall on San Antonio's northeast side—that he'd originally planned to resell. The initial purchase wasn't related to Rackspace at all, but it would become a game changer for both the company and evacuees.

When Hurricane Katrina struck, Graham was on his way to a meeting with Judy McCarter, a woman who managed public relations at Rackspace. As Texas Public Radio played in his car, he heard about the thousands of evacuees coming to San Antonio. Feeling compelled to help, he came up with a plan to send a team of volunteers to Houston to assist with the evacuee effort. When Graham told Judy about this plan, she questioned why he'd send people to Houston. After all, Houston was the city people were desperately trying to leave. She had a point, but Graham still felt strongly about doing something to help. It was then that Judy suggested offering the mall as a temporary shelter for evacuees.

Game on.

Having been vacant for five years, the building was in very rough condition and not ideal for living purposes, even temporarily. Converting it into a shelter would mean a coordinated and Herculean effort of revamping the entire space, but between city and county resources and local businesses, it came together, including showers, a makeshift laundromat, a cafeteria, a medical center, and a childcare area. They even had a place for haircuts.

Once the ball got rolling, though, it rolled quickly. Everything from calling the mayor to turning the Montgomery Ward into a usable shelter happened in a day and a half. It was a remarkably fast turnaround, which is a testament to Graham's ability to seize opportunity. Although it may have seemed impossible, he was willing to jump in, offer what he had, and make things happen.

A DATABASE WITH A PURPOSE

Even though this endeavor started with a donated Montgomery Ward building, Rackers, being fanatical at heart, wanted to help with more. For example, when evacuees got off buses at shelters, Red Cross volunteers would greet them with clipboards and pens. Some didn't know or have all of the information that was needed, as they had left behind important documentation simply trying to escape New Orleans. And they were exhausted, many having not slept during the journey from New Orleans to San Antonio. All told, our software developers knew there was a faster, more efficient way to intake these vulnerable evacuees.

Rackers wanted to be part of the solution.

I spoke with Brett Elmendorf, who managed a group of technical Rackers at the time and was involved in the Katrina efforts. His team was also interested in helping, and as technologists, they had skills to offer that the Red Cross—which at this point was managing the shelter—didn't. That technical team worked around the clock to build a scrappy but invaluable web-based system that scraped all publicly available websites that included any information or intake from Hurricane Katrina evacuees, regardless of which city they'd been relocated to. Why? The goal was to aggregate all the information that already existed from missing persons websites or elsewhere so that families could find one another and reunite more quickly.

At that time, Brett and his team were unsure whether the system would work. It was all experimentation, and they were trying not to step on the toes of the Red Cross or local authorities. They were suddenly faced with a situation that they were uniquely qualified to improve, and in the spirit of innovation and goodwill, Rackers raised their hands and said yes. Yes to the vulnerable evacuees, yes to taking the risk, and yes to using the skills they had to pitch in and help. In the end, they handed the system that had helped so many over to the Red Cross.

This is a great example of how Rackers operate: often without a playbook but with tons of heart and a spirit of innovation to figure things out.

THE DATA ANGEL PROJECT

After the number of evacuees from Katrina decreased, the team was able to consolidate everyone who remained in San Antonio into one main shelter at a former Air Force base in San Antonio. Rackers created the database and system that helped at intake, but now the needs were changing. The consolidated shelter needed to restrict access to only those who were still taking refuge from the hurricane. Since Rackspace uses a secure photo badge ID system, it was relatively simple to create that same system for the tenants of the shelter. Each badge had the person's photo and information, and badges were eventually upgraded to include barcodes on the back, granting only approved tenants access to the building and adding a layer of efficiency in the process.

The impact of the badges grew: over time, the City of San Antonio allowed banks and other institutional organizations to recognize the badges as legitimate forms of ID for evacuees outside of the shelter. This may sound like a small act, but the outcomes were monumental. Brett told me the story of one gentleman who kept his whole life savings in a jar. He had brought the jar on the bus with him when he fled New Orleans, and he refused to put it down. He even slept on the jar. Understandably, he was guarding it with his life. This man used his newly issued ID badge to open a bank account and finally deposit the money he'd work so hard to save. He could literally sleep better at night because of what the badge enabled him to do.

Ultimately, the goal of Rackers working in the community was then and is now to bring a level of comfort and ability to others. Frequently during traumatic crises such as a natural disaster, accessing support systems requires having a legitimate government ID. Rackers couldn't fix the problem entirely—and weren't always sure how to make it happen—but they tried and used what they had. The "heart of a Racker" often means stepping in to support when a need arises, just saying yes.

Location-wise, for many Rackers, the Hurricane Katrina project was their first interaction with not only the mall itself but also with that area of San Antonio—an area that had a bit of a reputation for being a rough part of town. After all, the mall had shut down as a result of gang violence and the subsequent economic slowdown that a tarnished reputation brought with it. At the time, nobody expected Rackspace to move to the mall, as Graham had initially bought that building as an investment property for his real estate portfolio.

But that's not what happened.

OUR MOVE

Rackspace had been looking for a location for expansion, as the early 2000s were years of hypergrowth. After the shelter was cleared out, the city of Windcrest—a San Antonio suburb where the mall is technically located—approached Graham about buying the Montgomery Ward building from him. Their aim was to attract Nationwide Insurance to come to San Antonio, building the business pipeline in the area. When Nationwide said it needed only half of the space, the city offered the other half to Rackspace to rent. Because Rackspace was keen to expand anyway and had had some trouble finding a location that would meet all its needs, the board decided that, unconventional as it was, Rackspace would move into the mall.

The stakeholders took some convincing regarding the decision. Originally, the board discussed building a brand-new campus in the Texas Hill Country or even moving to another state. Silicon Valley and Raleigh, North Carolina, were options that would have been logical choices given their access to tech talent, but Graham, being the visionary that he is, declared that Rackspace wasn't just moving into a dead mall on the "wrong" side of town. The company would stay in San Antonio and create a beautiful campus that people would travel from around the world to see.

But the idea had its fair share of critics. A major pushback was that few Rackers wanted to work on that side of San Antonio, which was more socioeconomically challenged than Rackspace's location at the time. It was notorious for its rough reputation, and even though the mall itself definitely had enough square footage and parking to accommodate the growing business, IH-35 ran perpendicular to the mall so the area served more "function" than "form." And besides, how would Rackspace's customers view the company? The board of directors put up a hard fight against the idea of moving into the building. They struggled to see a vision for the mall. Luckily, Graham has always been a visionary. He worked with an innovative architect and drafted plans to help the board see what was possible.

The rest, as they say, is history.

THE RACKSPACE FOUNDATION BIRTH STORY: STARTING WITH SCHOOLS

Windsor Park Mall is located in an area that is both commercial and residential. It has lots of small businesses but few major players in the immediate area. Many of the businesses are made up of fast-food chain restaurants, title loan businesses, pawn shops, and discount retail stores. But more than anything, there are lots of neighborhoods and apartments, so schools also have a significant presence in the area. For example, Roosevelt High School is right next door to Rackspace. Rackers drive right by it when coming into work—they did then, and they do today. For that reason, schools have always been a part of their civic consciousness.

When the move was still fresh, the goal was to help alleviate employees' concerns about the area. The quickly growing tech company could have walled itself off from the community, but Graham had other plans: to double down, invest in the area, and transform it. As Graham told Rackers at the time, "We don't just want to be tenants on Walzem Road. We want to be true citizens here. And as we succeed, we'll raise this community up with us."

Considering all the stakeholders the company could have potentially worked with—including small business owners, neighborhood associations, and city and county officials—or even the option of simply going it alone, it seemed that the most obvious way to create community transformation was by starting with the numerous schools near Rackspace. In 2009, a Racker named Mari Aguirre helped Graham bring that vision to life and started the Rackspace Foundation, a separate-from-Rackspace 501(c)(3) organization, to do just that. She reached out to the schools and the school district's central office, introduced the company, and offered Rackspace's help.

Initially, Graham and Mari led the charge for school support. Like moving into an abandoned mall, it was an unconventional maneuver, not without its critics. Graham's argument was that everyone would remember Rackspace for transforming the area, and the idea inspired Mari to keep going. She knew it would be challenging, but it wasn't impossible.

Mari had done substantial research into other community transformations across the country, such as those at the Department of Education's Promise Neighborhoods program and the Harlem Children's Zone. They were all a bit different from what Rackspace was proposing, but they had one thing in common: effective community transformations that were centered on education. Because Rackspace was lucky to have a large number of schools around its global headquarters, it made sense to use the schools and education as our primary lever.

ONE STEP AT A TIME

As Mari approached the school district with ideas, the reactions varied. She tells me, for example, she remembers approaching Richard Middleton, the district's superintendent at the time, with the idea, and he couldn't say yes fast enough. Graham recalls getting a different reaction from the education leaders he spoke with—a "we'll believe it when we see it" type of response. Some schools seemed very eager at the beginning, and others were more cautiously optimistic. All were helpful and cooperative, though, and gave Rackspace a chance to see where this unconventional relationship might go.

A chance was what was truly needed, too. Rackspace did a lot of learning through experience, so in some ways, this approach was not new territory. Creating a plan along the way, moving one step at a time, was really the only option. As in many of Rackspace's endeavors, there was no predefined playbook for this model.

While big, bold moves are part of Rackspace's DNA, the initial meetings with the schools and district called for treading lightly. Although Rackers are obviously not educators by trade, it was clear that Rackspace had more to offer the partnership than just funding. As a global, billion-dollar tech company, it had the potential to bring something interesting to the table. Sure, there are practices and ways of working in the business that could be helpful for the partnership, but there are also elements that could be real game changers for these students, such as seeing what future jobs in technology might look like or having access to hundreds of volunteers.

At the same time, we've always been very respectful of the role of educators. We recognized then (and still do today) that educators are in the trenches. They understand their students and their communities. They know what will and will not work in their schools. Still, in early conversations, many educators were reluctant to tell us what they truly needed. They were willing to accept our help, but they were cautious about the type of relationship to have with us. Typically, school funding is cut and dried. It's transactional. We were breaking the mold, all the while asking them to break the mold with us, and that took time.

We started by focusing on listening instead of talking. In the end, the Rackspace Foundation would grow to sponsor seven schools and impact the lives of thousands of children.

BEING PRESENT

I often get asked why we chose seven schools, our Magnificent Seven. Some think seven is too many, while others think it isn't enough. Ten years later, I can wholeheartedly say that I agree with both.

Dr. Alicia Thomas, North East Independent School District's then-associate superintendent, championed the Rackspace Foundation's involvement and worked with Mari to choose the seven schools based on where we could make the most impact. As we didn't have a lot of data to begin with, Dr. Thomas was a true guiding force for bringing the appropriate schools into the foundation.

We started in one of the neediest schools in the district and in the chosen seven, Montgomery Elementary School. To give some context about Montgomery, its students live in areas straddling the city of San Antonio and parts of unincorporated Bexar County, meaning that some don't even have the benefit of city services such as garbage pickup. Housing in the area consists of many rental homes, trailer parks, and apartments. From the district's perspective, the school has the most need in terms of social services, improved academic achievement, and students' daily attendance. Montgomery's kids struggle, and they could use Rackspace's help first.

In Mari's words, "We went deep. We created Junior Achievement mentorships. We had reading buddies go into the school. We did culture work to create an engaging school environment and organized a rally for kids, families, and teachers on the first day of school. We provided teachers with shirts to show school pride. Basically, we tried to be as present as possible for Montgomery."

At the end of the year, the superintendent called Mari to congratulate the Rackspace Foundation on our efforts around school culture and investing in the community's kids. He talked about how the Rackspace Foundation's partnership could really be a game changer for schools in need of support and how he could see the evidence already. That phone call helped Mari realize that our work did truly matter to the kids and the community.

The Rackspace Foundation's initial momentum came from being so present in the first adopted school. After that, it was easier to generate buy-in. The foundation's nonprofit status had been awarded by the IRS, the first academic year of programming had been completed, and it was time to begin work with the other six schools. We officially made public our commitment to the seven schools, creating and signing a "Shared Community Compact" along with school leaders and district officials. We dubbed the adopted schools the Magnificent Seven because we wanted them to have a sense of feeling special. And Rackspace was getting exposure—through both word of mouth and the media. The *San Antonio Express-News* published an editorial piece that told the story of the Rackspace Foundation's work with the seven adopted schools, and it was aired on the local news as well. More and more Rackers realized that they could actually change people's lives, and they wanted in.

A GROWTH PHASE

After we created the foundation, got the district on board, and had at least one school that was fully on board, Mari approached the senior leaders in the business, including the founders of Rackspace, and discussed creative ways they could become involved. Although Graham was the foundation's visionary leader and champion, it would be more sustainable with a shared sense of support from the company's broader leadership team. Rackspace went public in 2008, so in another uncharted move, some of the founders donated stock to the foundation. The stock was then sold, which was a significant source of income for the foundation and propelled it into a growth phase. In addition, we created an option for employees to donate through payroll deductions.

The number of employees who signed up to support the Rackspace Foundation during our first donor drive was initially only around one hundred; even though that was only a single-digit percentage of our total employee population, it seemed like a lot at the time. But we also knew that financial sustainability was important to address from the beginning. How would we continue to cultivate new donors without risking Rackers becoming immune to the message?

The answer came in the form of the new-hire employee orientation program, otherwise known as Rookie Orientation or Rookie O. Since orientation was mandatory for all new employees, we had a bit of a captive audience, and it was important to demonstrate our values and our commitment to the community to those we were bringing into the organization as employees. The Rackspace Foundation was given a time slot every month during Rookie O, during which we'd tell the story of the foundation's beginning, what its mission was, and how these new Rackers could become a part of this community's transformation.

We were off! But as in all unmapped endeavors, we hit some bumps along the way.

HOW TO HELP

It's worth recognizing that there are different levels of help you can offer a school, and some are easier for schools to leverage than others. For example, it's easy for a school to request "things" for their students—notebooks, pencils, and the like. That type of support won't scare anyone off because there are typically known costs, quantities, and vendors. Additionally, the outcomes are pretty certain. If a child is in need of a backpack and someone provides them with one, it's easy to check that box and declare the need met. Furthermore, no one is likely to contest the outcome that a child's education was positively supported via the backpack.

It's much harder for schools to get help with more complex challenges such as food insecurity or family trauma. It's also much harder to address those problems, but we knew we wanted to go further and deeper than simply providing "things" to our neighborhood's kids.

During our first year, the needs we responded to were all anecdotally based. We gathered our evidence by having long, intense conversations with teachers and principals. Ironically, despite being part of a company that manages data, the foundation didn't quite know where to turn for additional strategic information—yet. As I'll share in Chapter 2, that would shortly change. However, the first year was all about trying to help where we identified a need.

Sometimes that approach worked well, and sometimes we missed the mark. For example, we put together a contest called "If You Can Dream It." The goal was to identify what teachers and students felt they truly needed to help create a culture of pride in the schools. We encouraged all the Magnificent Seven teachers to submit an idea that would cost up to $10,000 to implement in one or more of the schools, and we'd fund the best submissions at the elementary, middle, and high schools. What could go wrong?

Initially, the teachers were super excited about the contest because it was so open-ended. We soon realized that same open-endedness they loved was also a mistake on our part. Because teachers could propose anything from extra sets of books to creating a World Heritage Day, the submissions were all over the place. We felt like we had opened Pandora's box. Some ideas would reach an entire school in a surface-level way, and other ideas would reach ten kids in a deeply impactful way. How could we decide which was more important?

The bigger issue, however, was that we'd put ourselves in a terrible position: judging which ideas were worthwhile and which ones were not. The problem? They were *all* worthwhile in one way or another. Who were we to decide that helping to fund an afterschool step club was more or less impactful than providing audio speakers and microphones for family game nights at a school? Plus, we weren't in the schools interacting with the kids and seeing the needs and opportunities as the teachers did every day, so we didn't even have the context to know whether a proposal would be truly impactful or not. The decision process was a messy one, and we had brought the situation on ourselves. But we were already too far in when we realized our well-intended folly.

I remember standing on the auditorium stage at Roosevelt High School, announcing the contest, and thinking it would be simple. In my eyes, we'd be able to create community transformation by talking to our "customers." Customers first, right? Let the "market" tell you where to go? But it wasn't that simple. What we didn't realize at the time was that talking to schools, teachers, or parents would give us individual responses. What we needed at the time was more of a macro approach. Ultimately, we learned we were asking the right people the wrong questions. However, we needed to go through that experience in order to get it right.

In retrospect, even though we made program decisions (mostly) without data in the early years, what we gained was invaluable: relationship credibility. We demonstrated from the beginning that we were there in true partnership, that we and the schools were on equal footing as stakeholders who were invested in the kids.

WHAT'S NEXT?

After that experience, we decided we needed data to help guide us. We also learned that we needed some experts who could help us better understand this community quantitatively—from its roots to its current state and all the qualitative data in between. In Chapter 2, I'll share how the decision to bring in help changed the entire foundation for the better.

CHAPTER 2

FOCUSING SUPPORT
THE PATH FORWARD

Although we received a lot of valid subjective feedback from our initial efforts to help schools, it was difficult to make objective decisions about how to move forward. We'd devised a solid mechanism for support, but it didn't always address the problems directly. Furthermore, we learned how intertwined and complex problems, systems, needs, and opportunities are. For example, we were able to see the average attendance rate for each school, but we couldn't see why the attendance rates were what they were. We knew there were myriad reasons why a child may not get to school, but we didn't know which ones were most affecting our kids at any given time and which interventions we should support.

We could see if a student didn't have a pencil, and we could fix that problem easily. We couldn't see why, though. If the student doesn't have a pencil because her family was evicted last night and she slept in her parents' car, giving her a pencil wasn't helping as much as we thought it was. Too often, we found ourselves treating the symptoms instead of the problems.

Essentially, moving into our second year, we had passion and energy but lacked strategy. We developed programs based on anecdotal evidence and conversations. Our original intention for the foundation was ambitious at best and all over the place at worst. We weren't sure how to prioritize our funding beyond a qualitative approach. And we knew that being "all things to all people" wouldn't achieve the impact we truly desired. We had to understand the needs of the community more deeply, and that understanding had to be grounded in data. So we reached out for help.

A GAME CHANGER

As my team and I were having conversations about how we could engage with those who could help us understand the neighborhood better, Annie, one of my teammates, came across an article about Trinity University's Department of Urban Studies. Trinity's research sounded like just what we needed at the foundation, and, because Annie happened to have graduated from Trinity and had connections there, we had no problem reaching out for assistance.

We connected with Dr. Christine Drennon, who leads Trinity University's Department of Urban Studies. Our proposition seemed simple: As a corporate citizen in this community, we, the Rackspace Foundation, believe we can make a difference in our neighborhood, but we want to understand how to best do that. Will you help us?

We recognized what a huge, open-ended question we were asking. We knew our mission was to create a learning community where education is valued, families and educators are engaged, and students strive to reach their fullest potential. And we knew we wanted a research partner who could help us unpack the big questions regarding how to approach our mission, while also helping us understand the history, demographics, and statistics of those we were trying to help.

We wanted input from stakeholders and data-driven insights we could use to form the basis of a strategy that would serve as the core of conversation, planning, and coordination with our adopted schools and our nonprofit partners. But while we had a loose idea of what we were looking for, we weren't sure what form it would take. How would the foundation and Trinity's Department of Urban Studies partner, and what kind of deliverable were we really asking for? Although Dr. Drennon was excited about this prospective project, like our adopted schools, she had not previously partnered with a corporation in this way either. We were (again) in uncharted waters.

Dr. Drennon came back to us with a wonderful and unconventional idea: she suggested creating a class specifically for her twelve senior students, who would dedicate their focus to understanding the neighborhood. They'd learn about the community and its origins and analyze data such as demographic information, homeownership rates, census figures, and other publicly available information. In order to get quantitative data, they'd also interview a broad range of stakeholders: teachers, parents, school administrators, representatives from neighborhood associations, residents, law enforcement officers, business owners, school alumni, and even Rackers themselves who lived in the area. Why Rackers? Ultimately, we wanted more of them to move to the neighborhood, thereby creating economic and experiential scaffolding. We wanted everyone to learn from one another, just like we were hoping to learn from the study and from the neighborhood.

We loved Dr. Drennon's idea. Not only would she help us better understand the community, but her students were also able to work on a real-world project that would actually have an impact on the foundation's mission. It was a win-win.

The study was to have multiple phases and take place over a couple of years, with each group of senior students building on the prior year's work. We wanted the students at Trinity to really sink their teeth into the research, rather than simply having a transactional relationship with the work. Conducting such a long study also gave the community a sign that we weren't going anywhere anytime soon. Instead, we were being thoughtful and intentional about the process. The most important voice in this undertaking was that of the community, and we were listening to it every step of the way.

The relationship with Trinity University became instrumental to us. Each semester, a Trinity student from the class joined my team as an intern, coming to the office every day to focus on their research and be immersed in the work. It was hands-on, experiential learning for the student and helpful to my team as well.

A QUEST FOR INSIGHT

While data was important to us, we knew that we weren't just looking for raw data. For example, we could collect data about the percentage of homeowners compared to home renters, but we were more interested in what that *meant* for the families. How do homeownership rates impact student mobility, for example? We were looking for insight, for meaning.

Overall, the study was valuable for a number of reasons. First, we were provided with data that confirmed some of our assumptions about the neighborhood based on what we'd seen anecdotally. Second, we were provided with new data that went far deeper than we expected it to. Perhaps most importantly, it provided a perspective from the bottom up, which would be key to how we would approach programming.

In this chapter, I'll share some key findings with you and not just for the sake of sharing our story. If you're a business executive or other leader interested in evaluating and implementing new ways to positively impact your community, you may not have the time, resources, or ability to commission a study on your local area. However, we've found that many of these insights are broadly true of any opportunity neighborhood. For example, when I speak to social workers and teachers who serve in socioeconomically distressed areas around the nation, I notice that we all have similar stories. We know kids who sleep on floors without mattresses. We've seen kids devour school lunches and hoard food because they don't know where their next meal will come from. In areas of poverty, these aren't unique experiences. My hope is you can take some of the insights we gained—including those that are positive—and apply them to your community investment practices.

STUDY FINDINGS

The Trinity University study forever changed the Rackspace Foundation and has helped it become the organization it is today. Here is a bit of what we learned.

ASSETS

In the study, and particularly with the focus groups, the conversations quickly turned to the area's challenges. What was interesting, though, is that the work Trinity did also deliberately hit on the community's strengths and assets—first. What was working for the area? And how could we capitalize on that, invest in it, and nurture it? Personally, that approach was one of the most insightful parts of the study for me. It helped me see the neighborhood through a balanced lens, and it also gave us a starting point for our programs. I think it also helped the participants in the study recognize and acknowledge what was going right. Not only was I able to see the challenges, but I could also clearly see assets on which we could build.

For example, one of the strongest assets the study identified was that the community had an exceptionally diverse student population, but more importantly, that diversity strengthened the neighborhood as a whole and contributed significantly to the second strongest asset in the community: student resilience. As the 2013 Trinity study stated:

> Students in the Magnificent Seven schools may be the most culturally and ethnically-"comfortable" students in our area—which is one of the most culturally and ethnically-"comfortable" places in Texas and the United States. This ethnic diversity has resulted in schools where over a dozen languages may be heard, yet students are at ease in the diversity. It has also created an environment and opportunity for teachers interested in multiculturalism and social justice through education to practice and perfect their craft.

We learned that because of this combination of strengths, an identity of the students and community began to emerge: that of being code switchers. Code-switching, which is the ability to communicate across cultural, ethnic, and often economic divides, is intrinsically understood and practiced by our students. As the Trinity study stated:

> Students develop an appreciation for and a comfort with the communication strategies—the *codes*—of numerous cultures, and thus are comfortable in diversity. It is a

skill and way of life that is becoming increasingly prized in a globalizing world—and in our rapidly globalizing city. And these students go to school next-door to one of the most sophisticated information-technology companies in the world, where, through *code*, information is created, stored, and shared.

Furthermore, we learned that international refugees from all over the world have been resettled in this community, so beyond simply contributing more diverse experiences to the area, students—both refugees and lifelong residents—are learning from one another, learning how to work together, and, in some cases, learning to overcome divisions because of their code-switching abilities. For example, classes may have two kids who come from tribes or countries that were once at war with each other. Now they sit together in the same classroom. You can imagine the challenges that may surface from this kind of situation, but to our kids, such interactions present an opportunity. As a result, the entire community benefits.

In addition, through the study we learned that many teachers found the challenging environment intrinsically rewarding and that they were working in these schools because they *wanted* to. Specifically, the Trinity study found that "a combination of the teaching challenge, the room for personal growth, and the student-teacher relationship makes teaching in these schools exceptionally rewarding."

Our teachers deliberately chose those hard schools because the opportunity for personal growth appealed to them. They thought it would make them better teachers. In addition, Trinity concluded that student-teacher relationships are based on social and cultural understanding, a level of relationship that develops only with time and intention. Because our teachers wanted to be there, they were investing in these types of relationships to truly benefit their kids. These were eye-opening realizations—and clearly rooted in opportunities for growth.

CHALLENGES

Of course, the study also shined light on the sorts of challenges faced by students in the neighborhood. At the elementary school level, we primarily found the following: a lack of adult presence and mentorship, a lack of social skills, a propensity for students to read below grade level, and chronic absenteeism.

At the middle school level, the biggest challenge identified was a conflict between the social skills acceptable in a classroom and those demonstrated in home environments. In this age group, we also recognized the strong need for positive adult role models as well as more exposure to engaging activities and experiences outside of the classroom.

At the high school level, the study found that our students struggled to find postgraduation options other than going to college or joining the military. When they needed an alternate path, the number of viable opportunities—or access to knowledge about viable opportunities—was limited. The study also found this age group in particular was getting mixed messages about how to productively use portable technologies, affecting their behavior in the classroom and beyond.

As we reviewed these challenges, we knew that whatever our approach would be, it should be rooted in the understanding that we were trying to build resilience in kids, not pretend that those challenging situations weren't affecting their educational experience. We wanted to level the playing field, not turn them off from school. We knew we wanted to help them succeed despite their struggles, while also embracing their identities in the process. We knew they had real experiences and achievements to be proud of, and we wanted our approach to build on that. We also knew that the teachers and administrators who chose to work in these schools were the true heroes and that the Rackspace Foundation, having the backing of a multibillion-dollar global corporation, wanted to be in their corner.

The next step was to figure out exactly how.

WHAT ARE WE REALLY TRYING TO DO?

Once we'd gathered information from the study, the next step was to use it productively.

In our initial meeting with Trinity, we essentially expressed everything that was on our minds without worrying about whether it made sense. We admitted that we weren't the experts in community transformation. In fact, we had no idea if it was even possible. We just had a sense that we could be more strategic and effective if we had some guidance. If employees were investing in a foundation designed to make an impact in the neighborhood around its headquarters, we needed to know how to actually make an impact.

As we went through our initial brain dump and got more and more mired in trying to figure out the "how" of our mission, Dr. Drennon asked us a question that underpinned everything else we were trying to sort out: "What are you really trying to do here?" Although we now have that answer, at the time, it was a real head-scratcher.

I looked back at our original charter, a lengthy list of the key performance indicators and challenges the foundation initially wanted to address; it was broad to say the least, including everything from chronic absenteeism to teenage pregnancy rates to issues with student mobility. Admittedly, the charter was ambitious. To add further complexity, research tells us that these challenges are often systemic and interlinked; it would be impossible to isolate any one factor without looking at the whole. Like a lot of people involved in social causes, I wanted to tackle "all the things." However, Dr. Drennon's question, coupled with the newfound insight we'd gleaned from the study, gave us the sense that we might need to narrow things down. In fact, in order to effect true change, we'd have to.

The question led to productive conversations about our mission statement and helped us clarify the purpose of the Rackspace Foundation. We needed to decide our role in relation to the community and the recipients of the funding. We needed a mechanism to help us shift from charity to impact. And we wanted our stakeholders—the students, parents, and teachers—to be at the center of the conversation. After taking these factors into consideration and many, many iterative dialogues, we revised our mission and purpose statement to the following:

The Foundation focuses on creating a learning community where education is valued, families and educators are engaged, and students strive to reach their fullest potential. The functional mission is financial and organizational support to nonprofits working with schools and helping them foster better results and to bring together stakeholders to focus on a unified sense of purpose. The Foundation believes in partnering with experts and providing resources to effect change rather than invent programs. When the Foundation delivers on its partnership mission effectively, it results in high expectations for learning, more engaged parents, positive campus attitude, better teacher and student attendance, and great exposure and recognition for our neighborhood schools.

PARTNER BENEFITS ABOUND

The Rackspace Foundation is the first of its kind.

I know because, along the way, members of the Trinity team said they would love to introduce us to somebody who was doing what we were doing. The problem? They couldn't find anybody. We are place-based rather than cause-based, which is unusual, and we have both a corporate (Rackspace) and employee (the Rackspace Foundation) funding side. It was also unusual that we took up residence in a neighborhood that was considered by many to be on the "wrong" side of town. In reality, we were writing the playbook as we went along, which was both terrifying and exhilarating.

As a result, the study became a real reference point for not only us but also our funding partners. It gave them a deep insight into what we were trying to do.

Another positive result of the study is that it helped us build capacity in our nonprofit partners. Knowing that we'd sorted out the types of programs we'd include in our portfolio, it was time to focus on program evaluation. We brought in an organization called Westat, a research firm that helped us create logic-model training for our nonprofit partners to help them create or better understand their theories of change. Essentially, it's an "if-then" style of planning: if we create a certain intervention or opportunity for our students, what kind of outcome will we see? For example, if a partner had a creative writing program that helped kids focus on character development twice a week for thirty weeks, the expected change might be higher engagement in reading and writing for students, fewer behavioral problems, and more positive creative expression.

Once each nonprofit partner completed this theory of change exercise, we could see the outcomes comprehensively. We could also see when organizations were (knowingly or unknowingly) driving toward the same or different outcomes, where we had gaps or overlaps in programs or evaluations, and how we could create a common standard of evaluation for all of our partners. In short, this process enabled us to move from seeing how each nonprofit partner was performing independently to seeing how the Rackspace Foundation was performing as a comprehensive portfolio of programs. We also began tracking outcomes year over year so that we could see long-term trends.

We led all of our nonprofit partners through this logic-model training. Not only did it help them recognize the value they bring as a unique piece of the puzzle, but it also helped them see the opportunity in what we were doing collectively. Such training further gives the foundation credibility in the sense that we can demonstrate the kind of change we are effecting and how we're addressing specific challenges at schools. In other words, we can show the ROI of the dollars invested.

In their proposals, partners tell us the outcomes their programs seek to create. They tell us what they're measuring, how they're measuring it, and how they're doing compared to the previous year, both quantitatively and qualitatively. In other words, a nonprofit can show—not only to the foundation's board but to any other funder—the impact it has at a school level. This is a big lever when it comes to attracting and retaining donors, and it's something I'll explore more deeply in Chapter 7.

A STEP IN THE RIGHT DIRECTION

Even though the study forced the foundation, in a good way, to reexamine its focus, it didn't cause us to stop everything we were doing or reverse every one of our processes. In fact, the opposite happened. If anything, the study was a confirmation that we were doing something right.

Personally, I felt a real sense of accountability to those kids, and I wanted to know that our actions *mattered*. I wanted confirmation that we weren't going down an ineffective or arbitrary path. For me, the confirmation offered by the study was monumental. We needed the study; it grounded us and has continued to be our North Star. It encouraged us to continue doing what we were doing and keep refining as we went along. On the other hand, it also confirmed what I already knew: I was not an expert, and this work shouldn't be done in a silo. What I think is the problem might not actually be the problem. What I think is the answer might not be the answer. This study freed up the Rackspace Foundation to be enablers and connectors rather than experts. While we are a piece of the puzzle, we are not the whole puzzle.

LABOR OF LOVE

I vividly remember my time as a first-year teacher in a small rural school in Floresville, Texas. Any first-year teacher knows what it's like to feel overwhelmed by managing a class of twenty children or more. For me, the feeling was intensified by being in a Title I school, seeing firsthand how children from low-income families are deeply affected by their circumstances. I struggled to cope with the stories the kids brought to me every day—stories of struggle, of living in poverty, and of dealing with situations that I was helpless to fix. I could see their potential; I could particularly see what they could be if they weren't carrying around so many adult problems on their small shoulders.

I bought my students clothes and shoes when their hand-me-downs were far too big for their frames, as well as hygiene items when they told me there were none at home. I did everything I could to reach out to their parents and encourage them, to show them what I saw in their children. I did my best to pour every ounce of energy I had into my students, making it a personal mission that they'd each feel nurtured and loved. As a coping mechanism, I looked at each day like its own mini-achievement. If I got through the day, that was a win. I was in survival mode.

Looking back, I'm not sure that was the right approach. I was young and inexperienced, and I had more empathy for my kids than I knew what to do with. I learned something from the Trinity study that even retroactively applied to my early teaching days. The data helped me recognize that the challenges students faced were rarely about lack of love but rather about survival. The parents loved their kids and wanted to give them everything, but they were also dealing with making ends (sometimes) meet, unemployment, addiction, family violence, homelessness, food insecurity, incarcerated family members, and emotional trauma. They were doing their best, and even then, sometimes the kids and the family as a whole didn't get all their physical, mental, and emotional needs met.

WHAT'S NEXT?

I didn't stay in a Title I school long. In fact, I was not long for teaching—not because I didn't love it but because my heart had been opened to what I might be able to do with my unnerving experience combined with my passion for children. As Desmond Tutu once famously said, "There comes a point where we need to stop just pulling people out of the river. We need to go upstream and find out why they're falling in." It was now my time to go upstream, and in Part II of this book, I'll share some lessons you can use for doing the same in your community.

PART II

YOUR COMPANY, "YOUR" SCHOOLS

CHAPTER 3

IT'S YOUR PLAYBOOK
THINKING STRATEGICALLY ABOUT YOUR INVOLVEMENT

In life, starting somewhere is always better than not starting at all. Whether you're looking to get into charity work or social investment, the *place* of entry is not critical; the *point* of entry is. In other words, take a step—any step—toward your purpose, the *point* of your work, rather than worrying about picking the perfect starting place.

Part of my motivation for creating this book was to compile the kinds of stories and advice that didn't exist in the early days of the Rackspace Foundation. Although it's both exhilarating and intimidating to attempt to put a structure around these processes, my goal is to outline some of these entry points for you to help inform your program.

First, it's important to acknowledge that no hand raised or step forward is too inconsequential, no hour volunteered is wasted, and no dollar amount is too small. Regardless of how much money or how many employees you have, there's something for everybody in this space: the space of giving.

LEARN AS YOU GO

As you mull over ideas about how to best give back, perhaps my biggest piece of advice in the initial phase is to understand that your journey will likely be iterative. Don't feel the pressure to get everything right the first time. Getting started is much more important than ensuring everything is perfect. You can always optimize the next time around, and, like many things in life, remember that there's no point at which you've "arrived," no matter how long you've been doing this work.

Not only *can* you learn as you go, but you *should* learn as you go. In our case, we definitely focused on how the community was responding to our efforts, and we also considered the response from our schools and from Rackspace employees. We took that feedback, and we made both tactical and strategic adjustments—a process that never really stops.

Don't get me wrong: I am a fan of strategy. Companies are typically rooted in structure and strategy, after all, and I strongly believe in the power of both. From experience, I also know it's no use to make a plan and stick to it all the way down the hill—even once you realize you're on the wrong hill to begin with.

In short, be intentional and strategic, but also embrace learning as you go. You can do all three. The Rackspace Foundation is proof of that.

TARGETING SUPPORT

At its core, all charity is well intentioned, but we can divide its mechanism into two main categories: cause-based support (e.g., education, health, arts and culture, environment, animals, etc.) or place-based support, which may serve one or more causes but focuses on a defined geographic scope. Both types of charity are valuable, and both have pros and cons. At the outset, however, it's important to consider which would be a better fit for your company.

CAUSE-BASED SUPPORT

A company that chooses a cause-based model of philanthropy invests time, resources, or money into just that—a cause. The cause doesn't have to be strategic, per se. It could simply be something close to the CEO's heart, or it could be as complex as meeting a need aligned with the organization's core business—for example, a pharmaceutical chain that funds community health organizations. Cause-based programs and, in particular, causes that just "feel" good to support are common starting points for companies. Companies often initially dip their toe into cause-based support through invitations from other business leaders to sponsor events, as a result of board seat placements, or in response to a giving request.

Being purely cause-based can create limitations for both public and private companies. Both shareholders and employees want confirmation of responsible resource use and a clear ROI. After all, businesses don't typically want to waste time or money, and there's no shortage of arguments for spending budgets differently.

Meaningful impact is subjective, which presents the main challenge of being cause-based. Community goodwill, though very real, is difficult to quantify, as is improving a company's reputation. If the organization simply wants to align its name with a charitable cause or perhaps to make a statement about embarking in philanthropy, nonstrategic cause-based support can be very effective. If, however, the organization has moved past the "public relations" stage and is truly aligning charitable causes with the core business—in other words, aiming to influence conditions that impact customers, future talent-recruiting efforts, or even supply chain practices—cause-based support can take a form that offers more easily measurable value and impact to stakeholders as part of a business's operations.

The flip side of choosing what to support is choosing what *not* to support. In fact, that choice can be one of the hardest decisions a cause-based company makes, which is why setting boundaries is incredibly important early on in any charitable initiative. In my experience, the most challenging requests to turn down are disease- and medical-related causes because they are so emotionally charged. Whether it's juvenile diabetes, children's cancer, addiction, or any other cause in that category, it's an impossible decision to put funding toward one such cause and not another. In Rackspace's case, we decided early on to use corporate dollars—separate from the foundation's dollars—to fund STEAM (science, tech, engineering, arts, and math) programs in the education sector in order to positively impact the number of technologists—particularly females and minorities—in the future talent pipeline.

PLACE-BASED SUPPORT

A company that chooses a place-based model of philanthropy invests time, resources, or money into just that—a place. More specifically, Rackspace's "place" is hyperlocal: the neighborhood around its global headquarters. In working with the adopted schools, there are STEAM programs that align with the core business; we would be remiss to ignore the opportunity that they provide to kids who live and go to school in such close proximity to a global tech company. However, as a true corporate citizen of the neighborhood, we are strongly committed to a place-based model. As Graham said in the early days of the foundation, "Rackspace is the only major corporation in our area, and as a result, we've really become part of the neighborhood. Some people say we're creating a new model, and maybe we are. But what we're really deciding to do is be part of our neighborhood, be a citizen of our part of town. And to make a difference here. To make it better."

THE CASE FOR PLACE-BASED

In Rackspace's position, it would be tone-deaf to move into a community without paying any attention to the needs of that community. Making a promise to be true citizens of the neighborhood—not just tenants of the area—was the way to be authentically invested in both word and deed.

Most low-income neighborhoods have exposure to citywide, countywide, statewide, and federally funded programs. Those assistance programs are typically formula-based. For example, if a family has X amount of income, they will receive X amount in subsidized housing.

Such a formulaic focus on low-income neighborhoods often treats people like products, particularly because these programs need to scale. Additionally, and for the right reasons, federal and state programs generally focus on basic needs. Anything above a basic need is, also rightly, the responsibility of the individual (though one might argue that even basic needs aren't sufficiently met through subsidization or assistance). The problem arises, however, when so much more of a young person's trajectory is influenced by factors beyond basic needs. The place where the

Rackspace Foundation really had an opportunity to make an impact, though, was in those "above basic needs" areas: access to more positive adult role models, engaging and enriched experiences, and childhood socialization.

If we think about this opportunity in terms of Maslow's hierarchy of needs, our kids were typically getting stuck at the first and second levels: physiological and safety needs. We were able to plug in not only at those levels but also at the third and fourth levels: love and belonging as well as esteem. Investing in these kids could help them move up the hierarchy toward the highest level, self-actualization—toward reaching their full potential.

The other advantage of this approach, in contrast to bureaucratic programs, is that the foundation created programs as an offering. They're not a mandate, a "given," or even an expectation. They are simply an offer—a bid, if you will—for kids' hearts and minds. For example, social workers are funded in all seven schools, but that doesn't mean every family has to take advantage of social work help. Creative writing programs, visual arts programs, coding programs, a chess club, mentorships, STEM clubs, and even a youth orchestra program are available. The idea is to create a broad offering of enrichment programs to address the needs that the Trinity study identified but also so that any student in the seven schools can find a program to get involved with.

The aim is to treat kids like humans who are capable of achieving their potential, and doing more than just meeting their basic needs. The foundation we created is all about making kids feel special and invested in. Every child is worthy of being in a club that helps them discover and celebrate their artistic skills, for example. This is especially true in a high-stakes testing environment, where enrichment activities are often the first to get sacrificed for needed tutoring time. We offer an atmosphere of dignity, hope, and positive identity that isn't always provided by bureaucratic programs and that wouldn't be possible without a place-based focus.

As employees make their daily commute through the neighborhood we serve, seeing the place makes the work feel more real. Rackers aren't just sending money to an anonymous person we'll never meet in hopes that it will be put to good use. Instead, we're helping our neighbors. If we're going to run a multibillion-dollar business in their neighborhood, we should see them. We should acknowledge their needs.

Once the snowball starts rolling, it doesn't stop. And while we always hoped to create a pipeline for student talent into the company, we are now literally employing people who grew up in the same neighborhood we work in. They were the beneficiaries of the Rackspace Foundation, and now they're gainfully employed and paying it forward for the next generation of kids. That gives us a real sense the model is working and benefiting those we aim to benefit.

WHY YOUTH?

We chose to work with youth primarily because of the number of schools in our neighborhood. In our vicinity, there are more than 7,000 kids who attend the seven schools; we made a decision based on numbers.

However, we also realized that if we said yes to our area's youth, we were saying no to funding many other groups: the homeless, the elderly, small businesses, law enforcement, and so forth. As much as we want to, we can't address all problems at once. We believed working with students and youth would create a lot of impact with a relatively straightforward target audience. The approach helps the foundation's work, too, as prospective and new employees enjoy the idea of supporting youth opportunity. We also knew that working with kids through the schools would have a ripple effect on teachers and families, thus multiplying the effects of the work.

The most attractive part about working with schools was the sense of structure baked into that approach. We'd be working with and supporting the experts, and practically speaking, the schools already have physical buildings, safe adults, schedules, and calendars—and most importantly, they share our agenda of helping kids. Without the structure that schools provide, the work would feel completely open-ended. It would be difficult to house programs, and the liability was one we were not able to take on. We also chose schools because that meant we could let the experts be the experts and use our expertise and funding to enhance what they were already doing.

STRUCTURING SUPPORT: THE INTERNAL TEAM

Part of our support for the adopted schools—specifically for STEAM programs—comes directly from Rackspace. Because these programs are aligned with Rackspace's core business, it's a no-brainer to fund them, but I want to be clear that Rackspace's funding for STEAM programs and the Rackspace Foundation's funding are two entirely separate funding sources. They just happen to overlap with some of the same recipients.

It is helpful, but not essential, to have both in your organization: funds that come from the business and are aligned with the business's goals, as well as a funding source that provides more flexibility to support and adapt to the needs of the community. That being said, not all companies have enough revenue to invest money back into the community. This is often the case with startups and growing companies, but it also happens with larger companies that don't feel ready to make those long-term investments.

Other companies give a portion of their revenue to a corporate foundation or otherwise outsource support, which is a decision we could've made. I know many companies that work with organizations such as United Way to essentially outsource or complement their charitable activities. There isn't a right or wrong in these kinds of situations; different solutions work for different companies. Rackspace wanted to keep the sourcing in-house. That way, decisions are more closely tied to the company, and the programs could flex with the business while being minimally disruptive to the nonprofit community. Additionally, in the foundation's case, being a separate entity from Rackspace provides more insulation against changes that regularly occur in the course of business, such as shifts in strategy, leadership, budgets, and so forth.

Furthermore, we felt that having an internally directed program would resonate internally, too. As of this writing, the average donation from employees is $16.36 per paycheck. The numbers vary; some employees donate $1 per paycheck, while others donate $200 a paycheck. All donations are accepted, whatever their point of entry, as participation in the foundation should be accessible, not unattainable. It helps that employees can donate and physically see where their investments are going, too. As a result, the in-house, place-based option allows employees to feel like they're a part of creating a real legacy in the neighborhood—and that's because they are. That's something we're all proud of, and it has helped the foundation become as successful as it is today.

HOW TO GET STARTED

In Rackspace's experience, corporate giving came first, and the foundation was created afterward as part of Rackspace's relocation of its headquarters. Again, although the order isn't essential, we found that it was much easier to begin giving on the corporate side and feel out the focus before creating an IRS-recognized nonprofit.

When we first began working with our neighborhood's schools, we initiated relatively straightforward projects such as beautification efforts, community gardens, murals, and so on, based on what the schools told us they'd like. We provided all the materials, energy, and time. Through this initial investment, we sent the message that we were there in service of the schools and kids, and we held many volunteer events over the summer in preparation for the next school year to begin. On the first day of school that first year, we had a huge rally with Rackspace volunteers to welcome all the kids and celebrate the start of the school year. As an added bonus, spending time and energy in the schools helped Rackers become emotionally invested. We then used that momentum to help rally Rackers around the Rackspace Foundation. Without that launchpad of Rackers, our work as a foundation wouldn't be a reality.

For you, note that your impetus to begin can be a top-down or bottom-up initiative. When we began, Rackspace had a very passionate employee base, many of whom were early on in their careers. This was around the time that millennials began entering the workforce, which one could argue also influenced the momentum of Rackspace's social consciousness. If they had an idea, nothing could stand in their way; Graham knew and supported that drive. Alternatively, perhaps you, as a leader in your company, recognize the far-reaching benefits of community investment. You're someone who makes things happen, so the process begins. Neither type of initiative is wrong; in fact, both are absolutely valid and should be leveraged.

No matter where your initiative gets its roots, you'll need to understand some basic principles if you're going to move from an idea to liftoff.

- **Educate yourself.** Around the time that the Rackspace Foundation was created, the Department of Education was launching Promise Neighborhoods grants in an effort to revitalize low-income neighborhoods. San Antonio was one of only five communities in the United States awarded a Promise Neighborhoods grant, and although the area around Rackspace was not part of the Promise zone, we could learn a great deal from being on the sidelines. During the foundation's setup, Mari had also observed the work of the Harlem Children's Zone, National League of Cities, and the Bill & Melinda Gates Foundation. This research helped her understand the landscape of going into a community. Essentially, she taught herself what to do. Anyone can do what Mari did, but there are some important elements to consider. First, look at your local situation and ask yourself—and others—what it needs. Do your research, seek out others who are doing the work you want to do, search publicly available data, or better yet, align yourself with a research organization that can give you access to data and guidance on how to interpret it. Above all, listen to what the community is telling you.

- **Be ready to present to management (and ready to listen).** If you're an employee reading this, don't be afraid to gather like-minded team members and present your idea to management. If you're in a management position, it's important to recognize that your employees may approach you with an idea to get your support, or they may just choose to jump in. Don't be surprised if you find out groups of employees have been incorporating volunteer projects into their team-building efforts. If this is the case, embrace that initiative and claim the goodness out of it. Help move the philanthropic effort forward, even if the idea changes over time. Your company will be better for it.

- **Form your team with intention.** If you're starting a foundation, you'll need a board. For us, having a variety of representation on the board is helpful when it comes to remembering *who* we're serving. It's no use to have a board consisting solely of people who sit in mahogany-lined offices. You need those people, yes, but not *only* those people. Our board is made up of people from all levels of the business and even former employees like myself, and we recruit those who can use their strengths to move the organization forward.

- **Leverage outside expertise.** As you're ideating on the type of support that works for your organization, don't be afraid to ask for help. If the Rackspace Foundation were to do anything differently, in fact, we likely would have looked to outside expertise sooner than we did. As you learned in the last chapter, the Trinity study changed our world and allowed us to do more good in our community. The bottom line? Ask for help, and let people help you—whatever that looks like.

- **Go deep.** As you create your roadmap, my advice is to focus on a smaller number of programs rather than spreading yourself too thin at the outset. When we set foot into our first elementary school, for example, we had few resources. We had to take a step back and reevaluate how we could do more; that meant honing our focus. It's no use "adopting" a school and not doing any good once there because you're managing more programs than you can handle. When in doubt, go narrow, but go deep.

- **Publicize your efforts.** When you're starting out, you and your team will likely be wearing many different hats. Don't work with blinders on; take care not to overlook publicizing your efforts, even if it's just on the company's social media pages, website, or within an internal newsletter. Note that there are different forms of publicity. Personally, I don't see much value in shouting your achievements through a megaphone for the sheer sake of recognition. However, there is extreme value in talking about your work with the intention of building social capital in the community you're aiming to serve. And on that note, building social capital often includes showing the impact you have in a community. However your company disseminates this knowledge—whether through operational reviews, all-hands meetings, dashboards, or bulletin boards—show the impact of this work. Be mindful that there will always be a naysayer when it comes to social investment. Don't let them control your narrative.

WHAT'S NEXT?

After you've formed your overall strategy and committed to starting, you may be wondering what to do next. At the foundation, we found the key to making an impact in local schools lies in leveraging out-of-school time and enrichment programs. In Chapter 4, we'll explore what that looks like and what you can learn.

CHAPTER 4

ENRICHMENT PROGRAMS
THE KEY TO MAKING A DIFFERENCE

In any low-income neighborhood, lots of kids are dealing with very adult problems. They are often prematurely exposed to a side of life other kids are privileged to avoid. These kids often don't have a choice in their circumstances, nor can they control their situations. Our goal is to mitigate those effects without overhauling the entire education system. We've found the best way to do that is through enrichment programs held outside normal school hours, but we didn't always think that way.

When we first began working with schools, in fact, we thought it best to support activities during school hours—classes, programs, and the like. We quickly found problems with that approach, though, as there are inherent time and systemic constraints associated with restructuring a school day. (Looking back, I'm sure there was more than one occasion during those early days when the principals wondered who we thought we were, coming into their schools and making "suggestions"!)

Additionally, we needed teachers to buy in and sponsor our proposed in-school programs. In reality, the last thing those teachers needed was for the Rackspace Foundation to arrive and ask for one more thing to manage, monitor, or maintain. Thankfully, we quickly found a better way, and it's become our bread and butter: supporting enrichment programs that allow groups to work within the structure of a school setting but outside those already jam-packed, critical school hours.

For our programs, there are no gates. The only ticket for entry is that the student attends one of the adopted schools. As long as they do, any program offered in their school is open to them. In addition, these enrichment programs are designed to level the playing field. We aren't just investing in scholarships for kids who plan to go to MIT, for example. The programs are for anyone, regardless of how high their grades are or how many absences they have.

Why was this distinction important? In life, most people want to back whomever they perceive is already the "winner"; it's a surer deal, right? In our case, there's a reason we funded schools on the "wrong" side of town. There's a reason we operate in a low-income neighborhood. High-performing schools, which typically correlate with higher-income neighborhoods, don't critically need our help; they oftentimes already have the resources the foundation is providing, whether through the school itself or from the families and communities they're in. They may want our enrichment programs, but they don't *need* them. Our schools, however, do—and our programs are working.

Let's take a look at why.

LEVELING THE PLAYING FIELD

To have kids fed, supervised, and enriched outside of the normal school day is a win-win for everybody. The schools get the programs they need without disrupting the actual school day, and students get access to a variety of cool, impactful programs and plenty of positive role models. During those programs, kids are learning new skills, developing social-emotional learning, and building positive identities in a low-pressure, fun environment. Ultimately, enrichment programs check a lot of "need" boxes we identified with the Trinity University study.

The time piece here is incredibly important because, in low-income neighborhoods, many families don't have discretionary income to pay for extended day care—and many parents don't have working hours that match the school day's hours. When students attend our programs, a few of which we'll explore in-depth shortly, working parents don't have to worry about finding somewhere for their kids to be—or face the alternative of leaving children unsupervised.

Besides physical safety, our enrichment programs are designed to be normalizing factors for kids who are at risk or living in poverty. These programs help build resilience and developmental assets in students who are often tasked with learning to move forward despite negative circumstances that are out of their control. This is important because students' self-esteem and self-identity are often heavily influenced by their environments. Enrichment programs help kids from low-income backgrounds have access to opportunities other kids might already have access to. These enrichment programs provide them with what most people would consider to be essential parts of childhood.

In short, through our enrichment programs, we send one loud and clear message to our participants: We don't just want you to survive. We want you to thrive and have an experience that serves you, because you deserve it.

EXAMPLE ENRICHMENT PROGRAMS

The Rackspace Foundation supports many enrichment programs in its adopted schools, often partnering with outside organizations and teams to bring these solutions to life for the kids. In the following list, I'll highlight just a few. Although this isn't a complete list of the foundation's partners, you get a good idea of the types of programs and the intention behind each.

- **Girlstart** is a free, weekly afterschool STEM club that encourages fourth- and fifth-grade girls to be "brave, creative, and curious." The organization focuses on project-based learning and also organizes a weeklong summer camp for girls to attend. Themes vary based on what's topical for elementary-aged girls. A couple of years ago, the club's theme was oceanography, and one of the projects challenged participants to design contraptions to protect endangered turtles' nests. Another year, the theme was called "Camp Hermione" in honor of the famed Harry Potter character, and the girls created catapults to learn about physics. Obviously, this club is designed to be fun, and themes are deliberately chosen for their relatability, but the real takeaways are the STEM skills that the girls get to explore and apply with their peers and the interest in STEM that it solidifies and advances for so many girls at a time in their lives when they are prone to lose interest or believe that STEM is primarily for boys. (www.girlstart.org)

- **Good Samaritan Community Services** hosts a six-week summer camp for middle school students known as Camp Good Sam. Each camp is themed around a relevant young adult novel and creates an immersive experience based on that theme. The one based on *A Wrinkle in Time*, for example, immersed the campers in the book's sci-fi setting and the battle of good versus evil, all while teaching them about history, discovery, and the powers of love and individuality. The goals of the camp are to keep kids engaged over the summer, prevent summer learning loss, encourage healthy decisions, and involve families—all of which are especially important for students in this age and socioeconomic group. (www.goodsamaritancommunityservices.org)

- **Gemini Ink** is a program rooted in creative writing meant to provide kids with a healthy way to understand their worlds. During the course of the year in Gemini Ink's afterschool creative writing club, students create an anthology of poems and stories they've written. Some are lighthearted and funny, some celebrate the uniqueness of each student and their life experience, and some are heartbreaking, revealing childhood trauma and other adverse experiences. Their families are invited to an end-of-year celebration in which each student stands and reads one of their pieces to the audience—complete with a microphone. This writing program not only develops an appreciation of writing as a craft but also gives students tools to positively and safely process their experiences while forming their own voices, positive identities, and connections.

- **YOSA (Youth Orchestras of San Antonio)** provides a program called YOSA Más, an intensive program that gives students in the adopted schools high-quality afterschool programming, including private lessons, sectional coaches, clinicians, teaching assistance, and tuition assistance for participation in YOSA Orchestras and Summer Symphony Camp. They also get help procuring costly musical instruments. Because of the rigor and elite nature of a student orchestral program, YOSA also opens doors for participants when it comes to applying for college scholarships. Our scholarship kids who participate in YOSA tend to have the most amazing stories. Many who have never been in an airport before suddenly have the opportunity to play internationally at historic theaters. For example, while writing this book, I received a handwritten letter from a high schooler named Hannah. She said she'd had a terrible week riddled with taking math quizzes, running in gym, having multiple projects due, and arguing with her best friend. But when she got the news that she'd been selected as a Rackspace Foundation YOSA Scholar, everything changed. It was a dream come true for her. "I knew that some of the other kids had it, but I never thought that I would now get the opportunity to get one-on-one lessons with such an amazing player *and* get to play with such an exciting orchestra." She also wrote to our CEO, thanking him "a billion times over" for the opportunity and saying that without her private cello tutor and "without this scholarship, I wouldn't be able to further my musical abilities." High school students can be a mixed bag, which makes letters like Hannah's all the more meaningful. It was clear that she truly understood and appreciated the significance of what she was being offered.

- **Communities in Schools (CIS)** embeds social workers in schools to support students and ensure they stay in school and achieve in life. Students who have been identified as needing extra help from a social worker, whether due to poverty, hunger, drugs and alcohol, bullying, teen pregnancy, family crisis, gangs, and violence or other adverse circumstances receive individualized support that is beyond the scope of what the school can provide. And to enhance the support of the social workers, students also can participate in InspireU, a workplace mentoring program in which students are paired with mentors at a participating company for monthly on-site visits. During the visit, students eat lunch and get to spend quality one-on-one time with their mentors, who are matched with them for all four years of high school. Rackspace added a special angle to InspireU, creating a Gallup CliftonStrengths session for the kids and mentors to help them understand their gifts and strengths from a young age, all delivered by one of Rackspace's Gallup-certified Strengths coaches. Why? Rackspace is a Strengths-based organization and has seen firsthand how operating from a Strengths mindset can maximize employees' potential. When kids are able to recognize what makes them unique, they can learn ways to apply those strengths to add value to the world. It goes further than that, though: to break the cycle of generational poverty, it's important to shatter the *lens* of poverty. We want kids to see beyond uninspiring jobs and actually picture themselves in fulfilling careers, doing what they love and applying those unique talents. We also wanted them to see Rackspace as a viable career option, and by bringing them into the office to observe how a technology firm operates, InspireU does that. Not only is the company in their neighborhood and therefore accessible to them, but it's also a cool working environment and adds a new dimension to what "work" could look like for them in the future.

- **College Advising Corps** is a national program that helps soon-to-be high school graduates navigate the college prep and application process. It places well-trained recent university graduates on-site at high schools as full-time college advisors. They help with tactical aspects, including hurdles like filling out the Free Application for Federal Student Aid (FAFSA), writing college essays, getting fee waivers for college-entrance standardized tests such as the SAT and ACT, and exploring financial aid options, while also helping bolster a college-readiness/college-bound culture in schools. The Rackspace Foundation's long-time partner Trinity University spearheads the program in San Antonio. College Advising Corps was important for us to include in the portfolio of programs because for many parents who did not go to college themselves, the application process can seem intimidating or even inaccessible; so much is unknown to them. For example, many of our kids don't think they would qualify for financial aid when they come from large families where the income is barely above the poverty line. In short, most high school kids aren't aware of what their parents' income means on a larger scale, and most don't have to be aware of it until postsecondary plans are on the table. In many cases, parents are uncomfortable sharing their income information with their children and don't want to fill out the required forms, which can easily derail a vulnerable student from pursuing higher education. For the myriad of reasons that may interfere with applying and attending university, College Advising Corps makes sure students know their options and that they have advocates to see them through the process.

PROGRAM PARAMETERS

Know that in creating community transformation, you don't have to start anything from the ground up. Any school has a robust existing structure in place, which makes it much easier for you to participate. They have your constituents (the kids you're trying to serve), the schedule, and the physical location and facilities. Leveraging out-of-school time and enrichment programs like the ones discussed earlier allows you to plug into what already exists and bolster what's already in motion.

Your approach can look many different ways: you can choose to work with a subset of students, one classroom, one grade level, an entire school, or a complete feeder pattern of schools from pre-K to graduation. That's your choice, depending on your appetite and resources. Whatever you choose, there are a few factors we've taken into consideration as we've continued to evaluate the effectiveness of our enrichment programs—and you should, too:

- **Involve the educators.** Be responsive to what the teachers and school leaders identify as true needs, even if they seem far-fetched at first. For example, one of our principals expressed a need for a program to help with character development, and they specifically suggested a golf program. The sport requires quiet determinism and self-reliance. It's a gracious competition. For a child who hasn't been taught how to mitigate impulse control, golf could be an excellent teacher. We would have never associated "golf" with "character development enrichment program," however, had we not asked the educators in the school for input. You don't have to accept every idea, but never be afraid to start a respectful conversation about honest-to-goodness needs.

- **Determine the dosage.** The number of programs you can implement depends equally on the appetite of the school, the student body, and your resources. As a funder, you have a responsibility to offer stability and continuity to students. Yes, programs may shrink and grow through intentional and data-based decision-making, but you can directly influence the number of students a program serves, the frequency of the program, and the longevity of a program simply by looking at supply (the funds you have available) and demand (the school's needs, the students' needs, etc.). In the Rackspace Foundation's portfolio, for example, our most expensive program is funding social workers through Communities in Schools, because that's where the students' greatest needs are. Case managers are on-site full time at each of our schools, and some schools have more than one case manager because of the need. Be intentional with dosage and consistency.

- **Be open to pivoting.** For many years, we funded a Summer Literacy Academy for our elementary schools because the district approached us and explained that many students were on the cusp of not passing the reading portion of the state exam. The Literacy Academy was a tool created to help elementary students avoid summer learning loss. As the years went on, the district said test scores had improved, and they no longer needed the heavy focus on literacy. They did, however, need a new focus on helping kids in science. So we switched to funding a summer STEM camp led by the teachers and held at one of the schools. Foundation funds paid for the curriculum and materials, a stipend for the teachers, and T-shirts for the campers. Does switching to STEM mean we solved the literacy issue? Absolutely not. It just means the needs of the students changed over time, and we pivoted. You will need to do the same to ensure you're always adding value, not just going through the motions.

- **Don't forget fun.** Although it can be easy to get caught up in the outcomes of enrichment programs, don't forget about fun. It seems obvious, but sometimes adults can forget that fun is extremely important to kids. For example, during the summer STEM academy, the leaders wanted to culminate the two-week camp with a trip to iFLY, an indoor flying experience similar to skydiving, so that the students could have an immersive physics experience. The academy's leader asked if we would consider underwriting the field trip. Why? iFLY is technically categorized as an entertainment expense, and the district's restrictions prohibit spending funds on entertainment. It seemed like such a backward way of thinking to imply that kids couldn't have any fun while learning, and I don't think the district meant to send that message; it just follows the rules around spending taxpayer dollars. At the same time, the experience gave me insight into how limiting state and federal funds are in terms of what they offer to kids. Research shows that kids learn through play, so let them. And be the enabler of fun.

ADDITIONAL WAYS TO HELP

While enrichment programs are our wheelhouse, we reach out to the community in other ways, too. Perhaps one of our following efforts will spark an idea for one of your own:

- **Putting social workers in schools.** We have social workers in all of our schools specifically to respond to needs as they arise. One year, a school may need interventions for anger management. The next year, many students may require help developing social skills. In addition to working with groups of students for a particular need or skill, they also help individual students with school supplies, uniforms, and even intense crises such as homelessness, family violence, addiction, suicide, or the loss of a parent. These social workers are adaptive and provide wraparound services for students to help them stay in school.

- **Organizing an annual Thanksgiving food drive.** This event is a big hit for employees, who can each donate $20 to the San Antonio Food Bank for a box of food to feed a needy family from the neighborhood. Inside the box are the fixings for not only an entire Thanksgiving meal but also extra staples such as cereal, spaghetti, and peanut butter. The boxes are designed to combat the real problem of food insecurity in the neighborhood, so we stuff them with extras and work with each school's family specialist to identify the students who would benefit from food assistance over the holiday break. The event itself is epic, with hundreds of volunteers cheering and dancing, as well as lines of cars waiting to get their food. For those families who come by bus or on foot, we arrange a taxi to take them home, as we don't want transportation to be an additional barrier to receiving supplemental food. The Thanksgiving food drive is the most beloved event Rackspace hosts each year, as it truly brings the families of the neighborhood together in celebration and allows employees to serve in a very hands-on way.

- **Hosting a first-day readiness and immunization clinic for back to school.** Since very early on when Rackspace moved into the neighborhood, we've organized a back-to-school fair for the kids. It started out as a school-supply event for families. However, along the way, we discovered many students weren't ready for school—not because they didn't have pencils and paper but because they didn't have access to the proper immunizations. In those early years, there were no nearby health clinics, and many families in the area don't have access to transportation, healthcare coverage, or knowledge about immunization schedule requirements. We partnered with a local health organization called CentroMed to provide students with the necessary immunizations and comprehensive health checkups ahead of the first day of school so that our kids would be school-ready on day one—another way of leveling the playing field for vulnerable kids. Not only that, but we've always endeavored to make the back-to-school fair fun; it is chock-full of carnival rides, games, giveaways, and backpacks stuffed with goodies.

- **Giving back to teachers, too.** Although many of our schools have the *structure* of a Parent Teacher Organization (PTO), they don't always have parents who have the time to volunteer or feel confident to lead as board members. While PTOs offer various means of programmatic support to schools and teachers, their support often extends to helping the school's teachers feel appreciated. Without a functioning PTO to plan it or a meaningful budget to execute it, Teacher Appreciation Week can often go unnoticed in schools. We want all our teachers to feel like the Rackspace Foundation is in their corner, so during Teacher Appreciation Week each year, we invite our beloved teachers to a happy hour complete with raffle prizes and other swag to celebrate all they do for our kids.

A SENSE OF PERSPECTIVE

I've shared many examples of what the foundation does and what we give to others, but we get so much more than we give. One thing you cannot ever quantify with this type of work in particular is the perspective you will gain along the way.

For me, that perspective came through a story one of our family specialists told me about a first grader she was helping. The little girl's mother was struggling to retain custody of this child. She had previously been incarcerated for prostitution and was completely out of money, but she was cleaning houses as often as possible so that they could stay in one of the motels along the highway when she could afford it. Otherwise, she and her six-year-old daughter were living out of their car. As a mother with a young daughter, my heart broke for this small family trying their best to keep it together and maintain as much normalcy as possible.

Around the time I learned about this family, I remember the air conditioner had stopped working in my house. For me, that was a real annoyance. I had to leave the windows and doors open because it was unbearably hot in my house, and mosquitoes were everywhere. My daughter and I were sweaty, itchy, and irritable. Then I thought of the mother who was regularly sleeping in her car with her daughter. I imagined how unsafe they must feel, how vigilant that mother needed to be through the long hours of the night. If I was uncomfortable, it hurt to imagine how they felt. I wondered if they slept with their windows rolled up to be safe and keep the mosquitoes out, or if they rolled them down to handle the South Texas heat and humidity: pick your poison.

Suddenly, my bum air conditioner didn't seem like such a big problem anymore. I was in a safe neighborhood. I had money to pay for the repair. I had family we could stay with in the meantime. My daughter wouldn't skip a beat in school. Life was relatively smooth and predictable for us. Gratitude filled my heart, along with an awareness of the privilege we hold. And I was incredibly grateful for the family specialist and social worker who were doing everything possible to help support this mother and daughter from our adopted schools. While we may not be able to solve all of that family's challenges, we were doing our part to help.

WHAT'S NEXT?

Enrichment programs bring value to students and communities, but they don't happen on their own. They are team efforts, and that team includes different stakeholders with different approaches, capabilities, and personalities. In Chapter 5, we'll discuss the value of knowing your school and the mindsets that go with that important work.

CHAPTER 5

KNOW YOUR SCHOOL(S)
WORKING WITH DISTRICTS, BUILDINGS, AND PEOPLE

Even if you have the best intentions, you can't go at this alone. You'll need people around you. You or some of your colleagues may be parents yourselves, have served on school committees, or otherwise have strong opinions about education. That's okay, and good even. That experience can provide helpful background as you move through this process. Take care, though, that those opinions don't lead to false assumptions that can cloud your judgment and cause you to turn away from the core problem.

Take, for example, literacy. If a school's literacy rate is lower than expected—and it often is in lower-income schools—people are quick to blame the teachers, the quality of books in schools, or even assign blame to students who "just don't care" or are judged to be deficient in one way or another, perhaps even lazy. However, the school itself often isn't where the problem lies. For example, if a child is coming to school hungry, their ability to learn will be compromised each and every day. If the parent works multiple jobs and isn't available to read to their child, reading skills will falter. The same is true if the child didn't attend pre-K or have exposure to a literacy-rich environment. In short, there are many possible reasons for literacy levels to be low in a school, and more often than not, teachers, students, and families are doing the best they can, given their circumstances. This approach looks at the problem as a lead that will take us somewhere deeper.

Similarly, a high number of teenage pregnancies aren't simply a result of a lack of sex education. They're more frequently related to socioeconomic conditions and lower income and education levels in that teen's family. Further, teens also need access to contraceptive and reproductive health services. As I stated before, in the early days of our work, there were no health clinics in the area, which is a very real barrier to preventing an unwanted pregnancy, regardless of the parents' ages. Last, teens need supportive, trusted adults who can help them make healthy choices about relationships, sex, and birth control. For example, if a teen experiences an unmet need for love and belonging and doesn't have a supportive adult who can help them identify a healthy way to get that need met, he or she may seek that connection in other ways, which could result in an unwanted pregnancy. As educators, parents, and community members, it's our responsibility to understand the real needs of those teenagers, rather than try to apply a simple solution to a complex problem.

STEP OUT OF YOUR BOX

To make the most impact, check your assumptions at the door. Keep in mind that the schools and communities you target for support might not be like those you know. If that's the case, visit those communities to get a better understanding. When immersing yourself in communities different from your own, keep an open mind. Be truly curious about what is driving certain behaviors and outcomes.

Recently, one of our social workers told me she was working with a family facing dire circumstances. Among other challenges, they simply didn't have enough food. Even though she'd been trying to offer them food assistance, the family would not answer the door if they saw her car. Although she knows they're undocumented, they're terrified of accepting help. While receiving assistance in itself would not split their family apart, they understandably don't want to take the chance of any one agency raising a flag to another agency and putting their family at risk. And regardless of your views on immigration, we can all agree that food insecurity for *any* child is unacceptable. But this family's situation begs the question: how do we send the message that school is a safe place, with people and programs to help families meet their basic needs?

The bottom line is that anybody's situation might be completely different from the way it looks. When working in these communities, it's important to be curious about the real reasons behind people's actions. Besides authentic curiosity, it's important to come in with a positive intention, too. Remember, if the goal is to help our kids, let's really help our kids, not just pick and choose how we feel good about helping.

TIPS FOR BUILDING RELATIONSHIP CAPITAL

Whatever initiative you're thinking of undertaking, you can't expect to enter into a new community and be accepted immediately. It takes time to build relationships and prove to members of a community—any community—that you are there with good intentions.

The same applies for schools. We aim to move from the perspective of charity to the perspective of partnership, but that takes time. When we started working with schools, for example, they were hesitant to report any problems with the programs we were funding. In their words, they loved our funding and our programs. If a program wasn't optimal, though, they wouldn't say anything because they didn't want to risk losing the funding, or worse, the relationship with a major corporation. That's the opposite of what we wanted. In this role, my goal has always been to establish trust from the beginning. A natural instinct for many people is to fear new relationships. I have always endeavored to move from fear-based relationships to trust-based relationships; if there's an issue, I want to fix it. One problem doesn't ruin a relationship. In fact, solving problems together is how relationships get stronger.

Part of building trust is avoiding the idea that you will walk into someone's life and fix their problems for them, particularly by providing monetary support. Although it's easy to think writing a check can help solve a problem, money is not always the answer. In most cases, relationships need to be formed to create long-lasting solutions to problems.

Instead of taking the "we're going to fix everything" approach, this model considers the role of funder as junior partners and learners. We state up front that we are ready to learn in any new relationship. We don't walk into schools and identify their problems for them. Instead, the goal is to understand and honor the work schools and teachers are already doing while simultaneously enabling them to do it more or better. Coming in as a thought partner and offering what you do have exudes respect and patience in all your interactions.

That said, there is a fine line between being helpful and being pushy. Similarly, there's a balance between acknowledging that you have resources without immediately opening your wallet. At the end of the day, in this model the role of a funder is to be an enabler, collectively finding solutions to problems by leveraging energy, creativity, and resources to problems that can be collectively identified. In many cases, the wisdom is already at the table. Teachers and school leaders know how their problems can be solved. In other cases, as a funder, you can offer new ways of thinking.

For example, school leaders often ask to have professional development sessions or off-site meetings at Rackspace's offices. They like the idea of being in a different physical space so as to get into a new headspace. Being off-site can make people feel special. Think how you can apply this insight to your situation: even if you don't have millions of dollars to give, maybe you have a space, or skills, you could offer. You might have a team in your company that could facilitate a group of teachers to think about a situation in a different way. The possibilities to help are endless.

CASE STUDY: THINKING OUTSIDE THE (MONEY) BOX

A few years ago, I was speaking to a social worker in one of our schools. She explained that the schools had a high number of refugees and asylees from various places, including countries in Africa and the Middle East. In some cases, students were from tribes that didn't have any formal education or schooling. For example, a child could chronologically be in fifth grade but have never attended school.

In addition, some kids were from warring tribes in their home country but were now in the same classroom. There was also a cultural divide, as many parents were unaccustomed to having female teachers. Unless you got close enough and curious enough, you would have no way of knowing about the difficult and complex situations faced by these communities.

Perhaps most challenging, though, was the language barrier. The social worker explained how helpless she felt about not being able to have proper parent-teacher conferences because of the language barrier. She felt conflicted that the parents were filling out forms without fully knowing what they were signing. I told her about Rackspace's diverse workforce and how there is an employee resource group called EAST, which is inclusive of all Asian and Middle Eastern Rackers and allies. I wasn't sure, but I thought reaching out to the group may be a way to help with her dilemma.

I asked the social worker for a list of all the languages for which she needed translators; there were six in total that went beyond the district's fifty-nine supported languages. Then we sent a message to members of EAST seeking employees who spoke those languages and asking if they'd be willing to volunteer some time to help translate. Not only were they able to translate forms, but some even attended parent-teacher conferences as well to help interpret in real time and facilitate meaningful dialogue between the parents and the school.

This story is important because we didn't walk into a school and announce that we would help with their language barriers. Instead, we got close. We listened. As willing learners, we were able to understand the sorts of challenges students, parents, and teachers face. That allowed us to think of creative ways to plug in and offer our assistance—all for free.

BREAKING THROUGH THE BUREAUCRACY

I treat our schools as customers because they are. The same lens should apply to your community programs. Think about how your customers deserve to be treated. Think about what makes them delighted and what creates loyalty and trust between you and your customers. Every day, I worked to earn trust because I knew that our schools could choose to opt out of the partnership at any time, just like a customer could. I also knew that to win the hearts and minds of the schools in the area is to win the hearts and minds of the community and the company's employees. Think of the work not as a perfunctory checking-of-the-box, but as a high-leverage strategy with triple-win results.

Even if there is a power dynamic on the surface, it's important to put that aside—for yourself and for your stakeholders and partners—as quickly as possible. That said, we must understand that as a large-scale system, education has become highly bureaucratic. In terms of scaling, efficiency, and cost-effectiveness, this makes sense. However, children aren't products. Children are individuals, but it can be challenging to see them as such in the broader context of the education system. When I expressed my frustrations to Graham about this years ago, he shared a phrase that, although I had heard it many times, really resonated that day: "It is what it is." The education system is bureaucratic. It just *is*, and we cannot change it, especially not as funders trying to collaborate with schools.

Additionally, schools are highly risk averse—as they should be. They're dealing with children, the most precious treasure of any community, and they are funded by taxpayers. Understandably, schools should not take chances and big leaps of faith without fully vetting the opportunity. And resources are scarce, so it's critical to maximize the return on time and investment.

Conversely, the tech industry in particular has a higher tolerance for risk-taking in the name of innovation, so in our case, those two very different mindsets had to be reconciled. In your case, you may be working with a school that is much more comfortable with risk and innovation than your organization is. If that's the case, you can still be an incredible enabler of progress. Let them show you the way and help you understand the "why" and the "how" as you journey together. It's important to be aware of and respectful of each organization's risk threshold and appetite for innovation. Neither is better or worse, but they must come together at a comfortable place for all parties.

CREATIVITY IN THE FACE OF BUREAUCRACY

The role of a teacher, educator, or school leader requires immense creativity. Teaching is a form of public service. Teachers believe in the future and their ability to impact the future for the better. Ultimately, they believe in kids and the value of education. And while the saying goes, "No teacher gets into the job for the salary," teachers should absolutely get paid much more than they do for their critical work.

Not only does teaching require a real sense of goodwill, but it also involves creativity, energy, passion, and commitment to the work. Truly dedicated teachers see the profession as a higher calling. Teachers inherently know what is best for their students. They know their kids and believe in them. As much as they want to do right by them, teachers are limited by time, space, and money, along with all the other factors and pressures that are part of our education system. It's not uncommon for teachers to invest their own money in order to get what they need to best do the job. I call this out because, as you consider working with schools, remember that teachers are not just educators. They also serve as social workers in schools. They look after their kids in so many more ways than what they sign up for when they get a teaching degree or certificate.

When I taught fourth grade in Floresville, a small town outside of San Antonio, many years ago, I had to get creative to take care of my students. For example, I taught a young boy named Jimmy, who will forever have a special place in my heart. His clothes rarely fit properly and were certainly never firsthand. Every day, he'd continually have to hitch up his jeans. He couldn't get through asking a question without his pants falling low and uncomfortably on his hips. It was a constant distraction for him. I don't know if the jeans were hand-me-downs or if the family could not afford a belt, but I imagine it was a combination of the two. After observing this and feeling his frustration, I went out and got Jimmy a belt. His eyes lit up when he saw this bit of relief coming his way, this one small thing that might help him feel more comfortable day in and day out.

One day, a little girl in my class that year came to school sobbing. She was an absolute wreck, and it broke my heart. Eventually, I found out that she'd come home from school the previous day to find her dad had sold all their furniture for drug money. They were already struggling just to make ends meet, and now her home had been turned upside down. From then, I began to notice she would hoard food when the class had celebrations or snacks, claiming she wasn't hungry but wanted to take the food home to eat later. What happens when a parent can't take care of their kids' basic needs because of addiction? I didn't know what to do, but I tried to do what I could. I went along with her story and made extra plates for her to take home because even though I couldn't fix her home life, I could help her keep her dignity intact. I knew she legitimately wasn't sure when she'd be getting her next meal, but by covering for her, at least her classmates wouldn't know the trauma she was going through. Her home life was in chaos.

I know teachers who leverage special skills within their classrooms for the benefit of students, too. For example, a teacher at one of our elementary schools is a master gardener, so she helped her students create a garden on campus that not only teaches them how nature and science work, but it also feeds them. Another educator—this time, a counselor in one of our elementary schools—is a mindfulness expert, and she helps her students build impulse control through breathing exercises. These teachers probably didn't list those skills on their résumés when they applied for the job, but they use what they have to help their students.

As a teacher—or, really, as a human—it's almost impossible not to be affected by such stories and such acts of decency. As Graham said, it is what it is: these communities are filled with kids facing adult-sized problems. Unfortunately, our education system, like most systems, was not built to be empathetic. The bureaucratic system needs a child to learn the skills and pass the state exam, even if that child has been evicted from their home, or is food insecure, or has a parent who was arrested last night. The entire education system just isn't set up to address the lives that many of our kids face.

That's where educators come in. They help save the world every day.

BUILDING YOUR TEAM

We know teachers are vital to kids and our mission to help them. As you navigate your ideas around philanthropy, keep in mind that there are other educators and support staff, too, with whom you may interface. Here's what you need to know:

- **Principals.** Think of principals as the crux of your partnership with a school because, ultimately, they are the gatekeepers. They have the power to invite you in or tell you to leave. You want the principals on your side. Due to the nature of the education system, principals are often put in a tough position. On the one hand, they have to manage a very bureaucratic system, which means they are keeping an eye on tactical issues such as attendance rates and safety, for example. On the other hand, principals are expected to be leaders, which means being transformational, inspirational, and able to share success stories. Luckily, most principals strive to put kids at the center of solutions and have their best interests at heart. Some are willing to think outside of the box a little more than others. At the foundation of this partnership is the ability to figure out a common language between two very different worlds—the education world and the corporate one—and to be aware of the systemic nuances of the sandbox you're asking to play in.

- **Teachers as "sponsors."** We learned very quickly that there are a lot of enrichment programs that cannot be brought to a school campus if a teacher or other staff member isn't willing to "sponsor" them—in other words, be willing to be the point of contact, the coordinator, and so on, especially if these happen outside of school time. A background-checked adult from the nonprofit organization might be leading the program, but there still needs to be someone from campus physically there with them, or even willing to offer up their classroom to host the program. The nature of an out-of-school-time program means you're requesting that a teacher stay at school longer, for no extra pay. How do you incentivize them to take on this added responsibility? Generally, it's by bringing in a program that the teacher believes in and values, one they know will ultimately help them achieve their goals with students. That's why teacher buy-in is crucial. Instead of constantly asking teachers to do more, we try to use the capacity we have and continue to leverage our collective creativity. (Side note: You can also offer a small stipend or even a gift card for their time and sponsorship. Think about what would incentivize you to take on an extra duty at work.)

- **Counselors and family specialists.** The first step to working with licensed professionals such as counselors and family specialists is finding out who they are and what role they play. We work with both in our schools, but the family specialists—and they may have a different title in your schools—are key players because they are the tie-in between home and school. These professionals know more about their kids and families than we ever will, and we like to tap into that genius. Both are well intentioned, but the fact is that because a counselor's role has evolved to that of a campus administrator, they are often heavily involved in campus support, often including test administration. In other words, broadly speaking, they have more hats to wear than a family specialist. At the end of the day, though, regardless of whom you're working with, it's imperative to get on their side. As a funder, you have a unique opportunity to enable their work; they're not working to enable you. Although there might be a power differential in funding, the real social capital is held by those in the school.

- **Support staff.** The support staff at schools are the people who will check you in at the door, who know how things really get done, and can make the work infinitely easier. If you're trying to get through to a particular teacher or get on the principal's calendar, they will help you. They are the gatekeepers of the ins and outs of the day-to-day operations of the school. You're going to need them, and often, so get to know them.

- **District administrators.** District administrators are huge customers in any philanthropic effort involving schools. You want their blessing because those are the people who will allow you to work with the schools in the first place. They also have a very broad view into the schools and the inner workings of state and district funds, as well as access to emerging research in education. They are the resources that can help elevate your work and investment from a one-off to a full-on coherent, programmatic scope.

- **Parents.** When attempting to work with a school, it can be easy to focus on the kids, teachers, and administrators so much that you forget you have another group of customers you're serving, too: parents. In almost any school, about 95 percent of engagement comes from about 5 percent of the parents. Still, you must meet every parent where they are. You'll encounter all sorts of interactions with parents: some may be positive, some negative, and others may never want to interact with you at all. Whatever the situation, know that at the end of the day, most of them are doing their best and want the best for their kids. Always be respectful and treat them with dignity.

AN IN-DEPTH LOOK: PARENTS ARE CUSTOMERS, TOO

Because parents are such core customers, let's break down those interactions more deeply. For example, one day I was wearing a Rackspace Foundation T-shirt out in San Antonio, and a parent approached me at the home improvement store to say thank you. His son was a member of YOSA and had recently traveled overseas—his first time on a plane—with the orchestra. From my shirt, he knew I was part of the group that helped fund the program and the trip for his child.

Occasionally, the opposite happens, and I interact with parents who don't agree with something we've offered. A few years ago, for example, a parent called to ask for a voucher for the annual Thanksgiving food drive. The problem? Her child didn't attend one of our adopted schools. This mother, who had previously been a recipient of the Thanksgiving food boxes, was counting on that assistance again this year for her family. When I spoke to her, she was upset and angry. She made accusations that the program was unfair and its regulations were discriminatory against her child. In reality, most of the vouchers were distributed through our adopted schools, but our partner, the San Antonio Food Bank, also distributed vouchers to other area agencies and organizations so that we could be more inclusive of the entire neighborhood, whether someone had school-aged children or not. It was a simple miscommunication, but the important takeaway for me was that in her mind, she was part of this neighborhood and knew that if there was a perceived injustice, she'd be able to call, and we'd answer. That instance showed me we were truly a part of the neighborhood, not just some ivory-towered, faceless organization.

While most experiences with parents are wonderful, there are times when you might be put in difficult positions. You might have to apologize for situations that aren't your fault to help make someone else's situation better.

In every interaction with a parent, whether positive or negative, keep one universal fact in mind: regardless of their neighborhood, zip code, or socioeconomic status, parents want what's best for their families and children. They will fight for that. Personally, even if I have to go through an unpleasant interaction, I love that parents are fighting for their kids. I have the utmost respect for parents who are putting every ounce of their effort into their children. If they want a Thanksgiving dinner for their family, I want to point them in a direction that will help them get it.

ENGAGING PARENTS

Even though we'd all love to believe that every school has a PTO, in reality, that's not the case. In some cases, families are giving every ounce of time and energy to their own immediate needs at hand—understandably—and don't have the capacity to add anything else to their plates. Jobs often take precedence, leaving families unable to participate in the hours that PTO volunteers are needed. In other cases, parents may feel they don't have the perceived skillset to help lead the organization, and without a PTO board, there's no PTO.

The implications of not having a PTO are that parents can't be as engaged in some of the decisions made at their children's schools. Parents may feel as though they're not being represented adequately or that they don't have a share of voice without a PTO. That doesn't mean they don't want to be involved, though. If parents can't be available via traditional routes such as the PTO, find other interesting ways to plug them in. Think about how to give them representation and make them feel like their presence is important at school.

For example, over the years, many of our programs have added a parental component. In Gemini Ink's creative writing program, kids work all year to compile an anthology of their writing. At the end of the year, a celebration is organized in which families are invited to come to the school and have dinner—funding for which is included in the grant—and each student gets up in front of the group with a microphone to read their poetry. The kids are referred to as authors, which is actually a big deal for third graders.

Events like this are special because families are invited to understand and appreciate their children's work, perhaps even to see a new side of their child—that of a *writer*. It gives insight into some of what's going on in kids' internal worlds. Such gatherings help break down the barriers that sometimes exist between schools and families, and the children feel special with their friends and family in the audience. Dinner is provided, usually something kid-friendly like pizza, and parents are encouraged to bring siblings, thereby knocking down two potential hurdles for families: food and childcare. Additionally, younger siblings get to see what their brothers and sisters have been working on all year and feel excited for when they'll be old enough to participate themselves.

The goal of family nights is to build a tighter bond between the parents, the schools, and the funder and to show families that they are appreciated. If parents didn't allow their kids to participate in these programs, none of the work would be possible. Naturally, we want the parents to know the value of what their kids are doing. And we really want the kids to have their moment in the limelight. None of those are possible without finding creative ways to get parents involved and knocking down their barriers to participation. Don't let the lack of a PTO be a barrier to creating an environment in which students thrive.

BUILDING TRUST

Some parents will be harder to engage with than others. In fact, there are many situational factors that contribute to parents not being engaged with schools: their prior experiences with school as children, their current circumstances, time constraints, or even simple disinterest. They may feel intimidated or even fearful. Some parents simply don't view school as an ally, thinking of it only as a place that puts one more thing on their plates.

As I've mentioned previously, in my region, one of our more topical issues is that there are a number of undocumented families. They may have lived here for years, but because of the political landscape, there's a new wariness around engaging with institutions, including schools, hospitals, law enforcement, and many social agencies. They are afraid of being split apart. A fearful parent will be less inclined to trust a system or a school than an individual, so a critical part of this community transformation includes one-on-one relationships, PTO or not. Although the enrichment programs are an important means to help kids, the people behind those programs really do the heavy lifting when it comes to building trust with families. Support them however you can.

POINTS TO REMEMBER

As you navigate building relationships with teachers, parents, and administrators, keep in mind the following lessons:

- **Remember that you are often an outsider in these communities.** Your outsider opinion is formed by your own experience, the media, and other influences in your community. Don't pretend that you know everything. As a funder, your job is to listen. Be a curious learner. Give your customers (the teachers, students, and families) an opportunity to influence the solution and buy into it.

- **Be present.** Once implemented, don't be afraid to pop in on your program to see how it's going. Qualitative data is important. Personally, I get a lot of information simply by watching how our programs are being enacted—how the content is being delivered, the engagement of the kids, the projects created, and even how well the programs are attended. Also, on-site visits create an opportunity to learn about the kids and make connections with them. I love when I see the same kids at different programs. As a bonus, on-site visits drive employee engagement within the portfolio of programs. For example, if an employee is unsure of the real value of their donation, a site visit will likely change their mind. Likewise, as a funder, if you ever need reassurance that you're making a difference, a site visit can likely change yours, too.

- **Invite them in.** Sometimes parents, students, and teachers want to know more about a neighboring company. They may not be clear on what you do or even who your company is. Inviting people into the office allows your company to be seen in a different way, as more than just a faceless name or logo. Remember, any relationship is a two-way street. If you are invited into schools, invite the schools into where you work. If you expect doors to open for you, you have to keep yours open, too.

- **Offer what you have.** Inviting people into your space may seem unnecessary or even unimportant, especially if you have an everyday, run-of-the-mill office space that could be in Anytown, USA. But there are hidden assets in your workplace. Perhaps it's a meeting room that teachers could use to have a creative planning session. Perhaps it's access to an HR person who could talk to students about something relevant to them, such as the role social media accounts play in job interviews. Or perhaps it's simply to provide a "career day" experience so kids can see what their futures might hold. What you have in your space may seem ordinary or even unremarkable to you, but to a school with which you're connecting, you may have something very valuable to offer.

- **Be nimble.** Agility is an important skill, and leveraging it can help you avoid the bureaucracy of the education system. Sometimes solving problems takes a system of approvals; sometimes, though—especially if you have strong relationships in place—it doesn't. At the end of the day, when a child has a need, the clock is ticking. Childhood moves at a lightning pace, despite our efforts to slow it down, and being nimble helps ensure you can do all you can to make every kid's childhood a good one. Remember, nobody should do this work alone. Partnerships are absolutely essential. Your purpose is to be a facilitator and to enable the good work.

WORKING WITH OTHER STAKEHOLDERS IN THE COMMUNITY

As you build your tribe of good, my advice is not to overlook the other businesses in the area. More often than not, they are eager to help, but they might not have been asked or know how or where to plug in. Here's how you can help them help you.

CREATE CONNECTIONS

The best way to offer guidance to businesses is to first build momentum in your own company. Once you have a structure set up, it's easier to persuade others to buy in and be part of your initiative.

Another big part of your role can be to connect other local businesses to the schools you work with. That way, schools aren't as dependent on only one funder. For example, I once received an email from a parent volunteer who told me about an event they were organizing. In order to increase parent participation at the event, they were hoping to serve a dinner of spaghetti, breadsticks, and salad.

Instead of directly underwriting the food for the event (which would have been easy enough, albeit transactional), I encouraged opening the door to a new partnership with Olive Garden, which was also located in the neighborhood. I helped the parent with her pitch to Olive Garden: introducing herself as a volunteer for a neighboring school, telling Olive Garden's management what the event aimed to achieve, and asking if the restaurant would join in our community-wide effort and sponsor the dinner. This angle clearly laid out that by sponsoring, Olive Garden would actually be part of a bigger endeavor, one that already has momentum. And by creating a working relationship, it would hopefully reduce some of the friction that can come about when asking for donations. In the end, the restaurant sponsored the dinner, and the school had another corporate sponsor it could lean on.

Alongside encouraging businesses to plug in, it's important to open the school community's eyes about tapping into different resources in the area. For example, if a school needs sandwiches for a teachers' luncheon, we could point the administration toward Subway. If it needs gardening tools for a community garden, a Home Depot is also in the neighborhood. Need financial literacy help for parents or students? There's a bank branch. The list goes on and on. Take a good look at what else, and who else, makes up your community, and build capacity within your efforts.

In this model, your role is not just that of a funder but also as a connector between community needs and the business economy that exists in the neighborhood, and much like the Olive Garden example, it's not always about the money. In-kind donations of goods, services, or time are just as valuable. Area businesses get to engage their employees in the community and build some positive brand recognition, and the community gets invested in new ways. It's a win-win.

ADVOCACY, NOT ONLY FUNDING

To many in the nonprofit world—a world of partners we'll cover in the next chapter—advocacy means lobbying or any kind of political involvement to gain influence. In these communities, we mean advocacy in a different way: advocating for a better reality for our families. We are advocating for kids to be at the center of solutions.

One of the ways advocacy can show up when you're investing in schools is by looking at systems. Many of our school systems were built for a reality different from the one many socioeconomically disadvantaged children experience. As systems typically are, they focus on efficiency and scalability, not necessarily on the humans that are affected by the systems. Our goal isn't to patch flawed systems together with duct tape and glue. Our goal is to solve problems for kids.

For example, some time ago, principals told me their school attendance was heavily impacted by the weather. In a neighborhood-based school in which few kids have access to bus services, one can see how a thunderstorm or morning freeze would affect the large number of students walking to school. In the state of Texas, schools do not receive reimbursement for bus services that travel within two miles of the school; kids within the two-mile radius are expected to walk or get dropped off. For students without consistent access to a reliable vehicle and/or an adult who can drive them, two miles is a long way to walk—and doubly long during inclement weather.

In addition, through the Trinity study, we were able to see a clear (not merely anecdotal) correlation between particularly adverse weather and school attendance. So for about two years, I proposed the funding of a bus that would help students who fell in the gap location-wise get to their respective schools. The theory was that the bus program would fund itself through the increase in average-daily-attendance funds that the school would receive as the result of improved attendance (in addition, obviously, to improved learning outcomes from students being on time and at school each day). Based on the data I could see, it was nothing more than an educated guess, but it was one I was willing to bet on.

Although the principals were excited about the program, district officials were less enthusiastic. They weren't comfortable offering a program on a trial basis that parents came to count on and then taking it away if it didn't show a material difference in attendance. There were also logistical concerns. For example, the district didn't have enough bus drivers to add additional routes. Furthermore, it would be difficult to work out timing with the bus routes given the number of buses used for multiple routes. They'd need to have enough time to complete the elementary school shift before the middle school shift, before the high school shift, and so on.

While I understood all the concerns, logistical and otherwise, all I could think about were the children. If the program *did* work, it would be a win-win.

As I was "persistently" advocating for the bus program, chances are that the district officials found me annoying. After all, who was I to come in and give advice on how they run their business? But I also felt strongly about not just accepting the status quo: that poorer schools would always have lower attendance rates, so we should just keep on incentivizing kids' individual attendance with pizza parties in hopes that maybe one day the situation would improve. This needed change on a systemic level. I also felt strongly about piloting new programs. If they didn't work, we could adjust course or go back to the old way. But if they did, well, we might actually see meaningful changes for our kids, changes that others could adopt. We had a responsibility to at least try.

And we did. Eventually, the district agreed to pilot the program.

I don't blame the officials for hesitating. In my heart, I firmly believe that when it comes down to it, every person is doing the best they can. If we had all the time, money, and energy in the world, things might look a little different. Unfortunately, resources are limited. We aren't dealing with easy solutions or making easy decisions, but whether we rely on ourselves, our team, outside businesses, or a combination of all three, we can still advocate for what matters.

That said, the questions of whether and how to advocate are complicated. Although promoting, proposing, and enabling ideas is critical, it's important to stay mindful of the relationship with a district, school, or partner. There's a delicate balance between enthusiastic promotion and understanding when to accept a particular state of affairs and move on. (I may have had to learn that the hard way.)

Remember that if a program has been implemented but hasn't performed well or has experienced consistent challenges, it's also worth advocating for a discussion. Through dialogue, you can either change the portfolio of services or advocate for a new service to be implemented, but the important part is for all stakeholders to be at the table, feeling that their input matters.

In any partnership, whether with a business or a school, it's important to understand one's role. However, it's equally important to understand when a partnership stops working or when an idea isn't as strong as it once was—or perhaps that it was good in theory but not in practice. At the end of the day, as much as you should understand your own endeavors and intentions, you should also know what your schools want and need and advocate for those equally. Find where those needs intersect with your abilities and the abilities of the community, and plant as many seeds as you can water.

WHAT'S NEXT?

Think about what you're really trying to achieve. What kind of relationships do you want to create? Do you want to be a passenger or the driver? Do you want to copilot? There's no pressure to make these decisions straight away. In fact, the relationships you create aren't the result of one decision. The kind of partnership you end up with is a result of small decisions throughout the process, but it's important to keep your goals in mind.

Make decisions that align with what you're trying to achieve. When you put relationships first, success will follow.

In Chapter 6, we'll discuss another kind of relationship that can be pivotal to your success: how to find and work well with nonprofit partners.

IT TAKES A (COORDINATED) VILLAGE
FINDING AND WORKING WITH PARTNERS

While schools and local businesses are important legs of the stool, there is another segment on which this model relies heavily: nonprofit partners. Funders could not implement the breadth or quality of programs without them. Day in and day out, nonprofits are the ones on the ground, doing the work and executing the programs. They are experts at what they do and know exactly how to do it effectively. Nonprofit partners supply the content, curriculum, and activities you want or need to enrich student experiences in your adopted schools.

As a funder, it's important to come in with ideas. However, to execute those ideas and make them a reality, you'll need to rely on people who already work with students in those capacities. Here, we'll explore how to work with these partners and what lessons you can take away to apply to your own projects.

CREATING YOUR VILLAGE

You'll encounter many decisions as you look to bring on nonprofit partners. In all your decisions, exercise a combination of realism and flexibility. For example, in our early years, we had a couple of situations in which we thought we could rely solely on our employees to volunteer in a given capacity—say, as reading buddies. That would be our enrichment program. The reality, however, is that employees are first and foremost obligated to their day jobs. We all know schedules can change because of the shifting needs of a business. Meetings pop up unexpectedly, and project timelines can sometimes turn on a dime. When this happened, an employee would have to cancel a visit with their reading buddy student, sometimes with very little advance notice, which creates disappointment for both student and employee. This is not the "customer experience" we wanted to create for our kids or our schools.

As such, we learned that programs shouldn't hinge on our employees. Programs should operate independently of the time and resource ebbs and flows happening inside the company, which, as you'll remember, was one of the primary reasons we set up a foundation as opposed to simply making corporate donations. Consequently, we looked for nonprofit partners that could help us implement and execute programs. Rather than having Rackers go into schools and teach kids about a subject, we wanted "suppliers," if you will, who were well versed not only in those subjects but also in the delivery of that expertise to students. When we reached out for help, our program success improved exponentially.

Self-awareness is a crucial skill in any partnership. It's important to be flexible and realize there are experts in the field who are better than you might be. Be the facilitator. Fund them to do what they do well. Then stand back and witness the magic.

Here are additional considerations to keep in mind as you create your village.

- **Prioritize quality.** Obviously, you never want to fund a subpar program. But the question is, how do you know if a program or nonprofit is of high quality? First, do your due diligence. In Texas, and in San Antonio, we have incredible networks such as UP Partnership and TXPOST (Texas Partnership for Out of School Time) that help with impact/outcome data and program evaluation, so you might check around for similar networks in your area. Second, ask around. The schools often know of great programs, and even more frequently, nonprofit leaders can tell you who is doing groundbreaking work or whom they have experience with. You can check with your local community foundation or with a resource such as United Way. It's also wise to check online resources such as GuideStar or Charity Navigator for information about the nonprofit's evaluation or tax filings to get a sense of its operations. Finally, a good old-fashioned site visit will tell you much of what you need to know. Although informal, it will give you a sense of how they operate, how well they are attended (i.e., how engaged kids are), and what kind of content they deliver. Prioritizing quality is absolutely imperative and listed first for a reason.

- **Aim to fund programs that meet a real (not just perceived) need.** Begin with the outcome in mind. You know you want to work with a quality organization, yes. As you vet, though, don't lose sight of the bigger picture: What core need are you meeting through this partnership? Whether you've learned about this need through qualitative or quantitative means, that answer should be clear from the beginning.

- **Be diligent as you navigate your selection of non-profits.** If a nonprofit is experiencing organizational or financial challenges, it may be worth waiting until those challenges are sorted out before engaging it to go into a school. When investing in a community, you put your brand alongside that community as well as alongside any nonprofit you recommend. Bring in a partner you are proud and confident to stand beside.

- **Remember that you are a subject-matter expert in your own right, not just a wallet.** As a funder, you know (or you'll begin to understand) what's happening in your community and with various nonprofits. Coming from a business background, you bring different skillsets to the table that are relevant to your organization—perhaps a focus on customer service, innovation, or operational efficiency. You also bring the skills specific to your industry, whether it be technology, manufacturing, or health. As someone who is employed by a corporation in your industry, you're bringing a valuable skillset to the table, which is different from that of a school. Use it.

- **Explore all the potential fits.** It's critical to check with all parties involved before you put any new initiative into place, whether that's to understand current or prior partnerships or to ensure that the need is being properly met. For example, when seeking a nonprofit partner that could provide mental health services to students, the district said it needed an organization that offered the services of licensed professional counselors (LPCs), not just licensed clinical social workers (LCSWs), to meet our kids' needs. Although those designations sound similar, they differ in training and approach, and one would better meet our kids' mental health needs than the other. Had we not engaged in that conversation, we wouldn't have known to include such specificity in the request for proposal (RFP) requirements. Always do your homework, particularly when you're working outside your area of expertise.

- **Be flexible.** If you want to optimize programs, you need to be flexible enough to make shifts and changes. For example, we started our program for creative writing in two of our elementary schools. Soon, we realized it wasn't a fit with one of the schools, so we shifted it into a third site, this time a middle school where we thought it might be a better match. The nonprofit lost no funding because it was still providing services to two different schools, and we weren't forcing a partnership in a school where it didn't fit. The bottom line? Often, optimizing programs is about making small shifts to create major change. To ensure we're agile enough to do this, we keep an open line of communication with our partners, regardless of whether their programs run during the summer or the school year. We always want to be responsive to real-time changes or needs that inevitably come up.

- **Address what appear to be the "little things."** Most nonprofits have very limited resources, and the resources they do have are typically spent on direct programming costs.

In the planning phase, consider the A-to-Z experience for the nonprofit and school, which may include often-overlooked necessities like transportation or food in order to really make those programs take hold. Instead of creating additional financial or logistical challenges for schools and nonprofits to overcome, recognize those comprehensive needs and roll in additional funding to meet them. For example, if you partner with a nonprofit to run an afterschool program, it's likely neither the district nor the organization has funding to provide snacks to all the children participating. Yet once school is out, kids' brains need fuel to stay engaged. As a funder, you have the honor of helping make programs stickier, more seamless, and better by considering the extra details that make a program great.

- **Look at the big picture.** Think about each program and each partnership comprehensively. For example, instead of funding a nine-month program in a school, consider how the program fits into your larger mission. Would a six-month program with professional development funding for facilitators better serve the students? What about a year-round program or something during school breaks? Also, examine how your programs work together and enhance one another or the education experience of your kids and families. Could you take a vertical approach so that kids can continue participating as they move through each grade? As partners, look at all the facets—time, space, frequency, duration, and intent—and contribute your perspective as an outsider with outside thinking.

- **Build it, and they will come.** Think about every program as more than a singular one, and look at a nonprofit in its entirety. The more you understand what a nonprofit partner can offer, the better opportunities you can offer to enrich the students. For example, we funded Communities in Schools of San Antonio for many years before discovering that it offers a program called "XY-Zone," which is a male-mentoring and leadership development program for at-risk boys. At our adopted high school, the vast majority of XY-Zone boys are African American, so we connected them with Rackspace's employee resource group for African American employees and allies. We didn't know exactly how this connection would play out, but we knew it was worth a conversation about what could be. The result? The XY-Zone boys had an opportunity to interact with men who looked like them working in technology, so they could see themselves in technology. They were encouraged to pursue a future in tech, despite minorities being underrepresented in the industry, cultural messages and systemic challenges that keep these boys from reaching their potential, and other nuances that only someone from their background and experience could understand. We did not know there would be such a unique way for members of the resource group to support these young men. Yet when we started looking at the breadth of programs our nonprofit partners offered, the opportunities began to unfold.

- **Have a relationship, not a transaction.** When it comes to schools and nonprofit partners, you need to cultivate and maintain a fluid, mutually responsive, and respectful way of communicating. In other words, you have to trust one another enough to tell the truth. If a partner feels something isn't working, you want them to feel comfortable coming to you to ask for help without wondering if you're going to pull their funding. If there is an idea they believe you could help with, you want them to voice it. Likewise, you want to be able to have honest and genuine conversations about what's working or not working, or what you can and can't do with or for your partners. This level of trust only comes with time, so be cognizant of building trust as the primary goal of your partnerships.

ALL ABOUT RESULTS

None of this work is worth doing if we're not actually helping kids. A key prerequisite of our work with nonprofits is that they have the ability to detail what they will measure and how they will measure it, beginning in the proposal phase. Then, throughout the funding relationship, we have periodic checkpoints—not in a "Big Brother" way but in a way that lets them know we're ready to shift in the best interest of our students, should we need to. During these check-ins, we don't only ask them about quantitative results; we also want feedback from participants and stakeholders. Often, this anecdotal feedback is the most telling.

This feedback loop is a two-way street. Nonprofits should also reach out to school leaders and ask how programs are working. Equally, strive to ensure your nonprofit providers are getting everything they need from principals or administrators in order to run the most effective program possible. After all, partners should feel included in the school, that they have enough space and support to succeed.

These check-ins allow small grievances to get resolved without turning into a fire. For example, I once was told by a school leader that after a certain program finished for the day, the teacher's classroom was left a mess. Understandably, the teacher was conflicted. She was kindly offering her classroom to be used, but she expected it to be returned in the condition it was given. Problems like this are relatively easy to solve, but if they go unresolved, they can manifest into frustration, resentment, or worse, opting out. We simply communicated the issue to the nonprofit partner, which quickly made adjustments to ensure the classroom was left just how it was found each time the program met. No harm, no foul.

MEASURING RESPONSIBLY

All organizations want communication to be clear and consistent, especially when it comes to measuring results. What happens, though, when the area around measurement is inherently gray?

A few years ago, one of the nonprofits in our portfolio listed one of their program metrics as "helping kids think more creatively." The nonprofit was arts-based, so I understand the value they placed on thinking creatively—and they were right. However, that is a very difficult metric to measure. How does one determine whether kids are thinking more or less creatively than before they entered the program? And who gets to judge that?

To a group of artists, examining metrics like attendance, behavior, and grades felt too rigid. We worked with them to strike a balance: after a discussion, the nonprofit introduced pre-program and post-program surveys in order to measure how each student viewed their own thinking skills.

At the end of the day, even this data isn't black and white. When kids are self-reporting, they are reflecting on their own progress, which helps them build self-awareness. If you ask me, for a kid to even recognize that they are thinking more creatively already demonstrates self-confidence. After we unpacked this with the nonprofit, we were all comfortable with the self-reporting as a metric, even though it fell into a gray area. Gray is okay as long as it makes sense to everyone and contributes to the larger mission.

DATA

In my experience, data is both comforting and terrifying. And essential. The questions I grappled with in the early days were less along the lines of "What happened as a result of this program?" and more along the lines of "But how do I KNOW that this program directly and solely contributed to this outcome? What about all the other factors?" If you are like me and have an inordinate need for logic and certainty, allow me to let you off the hook a bit.

First, it's virtually impossible to isolate and credit one intervention for a particular outcome. Think of it like your health: if you are ill and are prescribed to take antibiotics, and your ailment goes away after taking the antibiotics, chances are the medication was helpful but not the only factor in your healing. There's also your overall health, your diet, your environment, your health history, your exercise regimen, and even your mental well-being. There's also the quality of antibiotics, the potency, the duration, and myriad other factors that go into "crediting" the medication for resolving the ailment. It's virtually impossible to home in on just how much each factor influenced the resolution. But the key is that it was resolved and in no small part due to the medicine.

Social investing is no different. There are so many factors that influence a student's success. So many ways in which children are positively and negatively impacted by their ability to get their needs met (or not), the resources they have or don't have access to, and the willingness and ability of others to show those kids that they matter. There is no silver bullet.

That said, not having a total ability to resolve a community's challenges does not absolve you from doing your part. As Theodore Roosevelt said, "Do what you can, with what you have, where you are."

Which brings me back to data. You may only have access to something as simple as the number of times a program occurred over the course of a year. Or you may have a robust data-sharing agreement with a district that allows insight into every tick of the impact-o-meter...whichever impact-o-meter you're watching. Either way, use what you have to tell the story. If your data is solely made up of poems that kids created at the afterschool poetry club that you funded, tell the story of self-exploration and creative writing. If you have granular data on attendance, behavior, and grades, tell the story of how your program correlates to those outcomes, and make a plan for next year based on this year's data. Start somewhere, and tell the story that you have. Over time, the data you have will lead you to the data that you'll want to pursue next.

QUALITATIVE VERSUS QUANTITATIVE DATA

In my experience, gathering qualitative data is one of the easiest parts of evaluation. Whenever we ask nonprofits for qualitative evidence of their success, they jump at the opportunity to tell us stories about kids and show the projects they've created over the course of a program.

Although qualitative data isn't an objective way to show success, it still has value. In many ways, the anecdotal evidence is just as valuable as the hard numerical data that measures attendance, behavior, and grades. Qualitative data also goes a long way toward building the narrative around your organization's mission. So gather the stories of impact, the student artwork, the writing samples, and the photographs; they will help you tell the story.

On the quantitative side, take reports from your nonprofits as another form of input, and don't be afraid to give guidance regarding the type of data you're looking for. We learned this the hard way; for years, we were not very prescriptive about what we wanted. At that time, we didn't focus on creating a comprehensive picture of the foundation's work, and we weren't looking at data over time. Eventually, though, we started asking questions about the substantial variability in reports and what we were really impacting. For example, some were reporting attendance rates, some were reporting competition scores, and some were reporting student self-evaluations. We had a whole host of other out*puts* that our partners were measuring. However, we didn't know the out*comes*. We knew about the activities each of our partners was doing but didn't know about their value or impact. While in the early years, these concerns weren't as important as just getting programs up and running, they became important as we gained ground and matured as an organization.

What I learned in this journey is that, at some point, it becomes important to make a conscious effort to help all of your grantees become more consistent with reporting in order to show your stakeholders the value of their investment. This doesn't mean we asked them to do any more work; it was simply different work and, for some, a bit of a different way of thinking about programs. And to facilitate a consistent approach, we offered training on measuring outcomes via a logic model and instituting an easy-to-follow annual review process. The process of offering capacity-building training for nonprofit partners is not something that you may undertake early on or even at all, but it certainly helps them to understand what you're looking for, build comradery among the portfolio of partners, and helps them apply this type of thinking to other funding reports.

THE ANNUAL REVIEW

Before an annual review, every nonprofit partner is asked to submit a grant report that clarifies how they spent their money and what they were able to achieve. Each annual review follows a template that builds on itself every year, allowing trends and long-term data views to emerge. Not only does this approach help with creating succinct and broadly viewed program evaluation, but it also helps your board, who likely isn't in the weeds as much as you are, to see a macro-view of impact. At this stage, partners also give us a proposal for the following year, and they present anecdotal or qualitative evidence, such as student work, photos, testimonials, or other relevant information.

During the meeting, in addition to quantitative data about the program's impact, we also consider what the providing partner learned, how they may have pivoted midcourse, and any changes they (or we) propose for the following year. I also bring into consideration feedback from the school leaders—what they see as working or not working, assessing how well the program is meeting their students' needs, and whether there are any speed bumps that need to be smoothed out. Based on that discussion, we decide to continue, modify, or end each program.

WHAT'S NEXT?

As you navigate the world of nonprofit partners, don't forget why you're doing this: you're meeting a community's need. At every check-in and every opportunity, evaluate your current results against that intended outcome. Look at the evidence. Know what the school can contribute and what the nonprofit can contribute. Take data seriously. Don't be afraid to shift in service of the students.

In Chapter 7, we'll take a look at how to use your company's time and talent to drive and shape your support of schools and students.

CHAPTER 7

IN THE LONG RUN
MINING AND BINDING YOUR ORGANIZATION

When the Rackspace Foundation was started, there were about ninety employee donors. As of this writing, the foundation is nearing 2,000 donors—an amazing feat. Through their donations, over $6 million has been invested in the schools.

Over the years, we found that Rackspace employees naturally want to participate in programs. In 2019, almost 60 percent of the employees participated in some variety of the company's community-based initiatives, whether by way of volunteering or donations. In the United States, a given company's employee participation norm is 23 percent, and in the tech industry in particular, it is 35 percent. Rackspace surpassed all those figures.

We also saw a reliable, year-over-year correlation between participation in these programs and engagement scores. Rackspace employees who participated in community programs had a 12 percent higher engagement score in the workplace. Clearly, program participation has a material impact on the business. Programs such as these help make employees happier, more engaged, and more productive—plus, they help make a difference in communities.

This buy-in matters, and it was generated with intention. From the beginning of their journey, employees were given an opportunity to donate and become a part of the foundation's mission. During their new hire orientation process, we explained the foundation and the work the company did in the community, and we held donor events throughout the year to keep the excitement high.

As a general rule, people—your employees or otherwise—have either discretionary time or discretionary money. It's rare to have both. The higher up the ladder, the more appealing it is for an employee to set up something like an automatic payroll deduction in order to participate in a company's community investment programs. Because they often lack time, giving money works for them. On the flip side, many entry-level employees may not have the sort of discretionary income to donate every month. In that case, they're willing to offer their time. Both are valuable, and it's important to create entry points to your programs that are not one-size-fits-all.

The goal of community investment programs should be to provide employees with options, meet them wherever they are, and appreciate everything they contribute. And if your employees want to do even more, let them! There are endless opportunities for employees at every level to be influencers at the team, business unit, or company level. You might plug them in as champions for volunteer events, as internal or external presenters, or even as deputized extensions of your team so that they can create and lead community-based programs. By getting these people on board with your programs, they leverage your influence, and you leverage their time and passion. It's a win-win for both employees and the organization.

FROM BEAUTIFICATION TO HERE

When the foundation was first set up, we started with beautification projects in schools. That was before we had a real handle on what we were going to do and how to make it happen. All we knew was that schools would be our vehicles for community transformation.

Beautification included anything from landscaping projects to painting murals to building community gardens. Our goal was to refresh the school, give them a little love. Often, these projects would happen during the summer, so the teachers and students would come back to a revived campus.

As time went on, these projects evolved to support the curriculum. For example, one year we donated and installed monitors for one of our middle schools to be able to have video announcements. This gave everyone access to morning announcements all over campus, not just in the classrooms. We created a display case in the front hall with a monitor that served as a message board for students and families.

We continued to evolve. A couple of years later, when one of the middle schools requested an escape room as part of its technology curriculum, we jumped on board. The goal was for kids to learn about cracking codes and cybersecurity in a way that made sense for them, and it was a hit.

Our portfolio of projects continued to grow, and even though we refined it and our methods, the work still includes a reactive, or responsive, element. In fact, there's absolutely nothing wrong with having a level of responsivity in your portfolio, especially at the outset. Why? There are always unplanned opportunities that present themselves outside of your traditional funding cycle. Perhaps a young adult author is coming to town to speak, and there's an opportunity to bring them into one of the schools to speak. Or perhaps the ROTC team at one of your adopted schools has qualified to compete at the national level but doesn't have funds to travel. Both of these examples occurred during my time at the Rackspace Foundation, and both were exceptionally valuable to enhancing the school experience for our kids.

In socioeconomically depressed schools, there are plenty of opportunities for kids to participate, but the resources required to get them on a level playing field with other more resourced schools don't always exist. Responsive funds give you flexibility to meet those needs. They also give kids the message that they have a fighting chance, that when good things happen, they can jump in and say yes to the opportunity. Even if your efforts are reactive, if your goal is to normalize experiences and level the playing field, you're onto something.

WE ALL GIVE BACK DIFFERENTLY

In the media, we always hear about schools being underfunded. Obviously, extra funding wouldn't hurt, but what most people don't realize is that schools often need *humans* just as much as they need dollars. They need positive role models who can expose kids to different walks of life. Kids need to be surrounded by different skillsets, personalities, worldviews, backgrounds, and experiences. They need different flavors of hope.

I understand that companies may be unsure of how to get their employees involved in schools. The good news is that school districts have very clear guidelines and processes for working with students, so you can start by asking the school how to begin. From there, get input from the principal or school administrator regarding how your company's employees can be of service. Maybe the school needs something simple like reading buddies for kids, help executing a project, or even volunteers to point kids in the right direction on the first day of school so they don't get lost. In my experience, adults tend to overthink what "skills" they can bring to the table, when in reality, a warm, caring person is all that's required.

At the end of the day, when funding a program, writing a check is the most impersonal part. The human interaction is what solidifies a connection with a school. You want the staff to look you in the eye and know you're there for the right reasons. Equally, you want to look them in the eye and know you're helping them meet a genuine need—that your time, energy, and dollars are well spent.

That said, people choose to give back differently, and although there is no right or wrong way to contribute, there are ways to be more strategic about your involvement. Start by thinking about your company's biggest strength. Is it the culture? The expertise? The widgets you sell? How can you leverage that strength to benefit the broader community? What are your employees passionate about? What are they skilled in? Can you create space for them to use that passion or those skills for the greater good, all the while embedding a heart of service in your organization's culture?

Take care to really see your company for what it can offer, overlooking nothing. If you need help, ask others outside the organization what they see as special or unique about your company. Then look for where your assets overlap with the needs of the community—that's where the magic happens. It may not be obvious at first, but as your relationships with the community grow, your understanding of how you may be able to help will become clear.

TIPS FOR ACHIEVING RESULTS

At Rackspace, our donors and volunteers were the linchpins of our success. Here are a few tips that served us well.

- **Listen to what your employees care about.** Make an effort to understand your employee base. What do they want? Which causes matter to them? How do they prefer to give back? When people are invested in what they're doing, they give a little extra—that's just human nature. Leveraging the passion your employees already have makes giving back more successful, more intuitive, and more likely to take hold.

- **Create delighters.** Getting your employees invested in a community usually doesn't take a hard sell, but it's helpful if you include delighters to make the experience, well, delightful.** This could mean providing lunch during or after a volunteer project, giving them a volunteer T-shirt to wear, or even making the volunteer opportunity open to employees' families.

- **Include community involvement in the structure of your employees' experience.** A way to ensure that your organization keeps its social investment commitment is to designate a day when the whole office, or at least a large part, takes time to work on a planned

---

*Some delighters go over better than others, I might add. Once, when publicizing an event, I thought it would be fun to bring the marching band from Roosevelt High School to perform unannounced in the building. Who doesn't love a marching band? As it turns out, sales department members on live sales calls don't. Still, the kids were excited, and we definitely made an impression!

volunteer project, such as at your local food bank or animal shelter. Companies can also make volunteer time off (VTO) part of their benefits packages, giving employees a specific number of hours to use on volunteerism each year. Celebrate the employees who use their VTO, and highlight their efforts in regular company-wide meetings or communications. For example, we had an employee resources group called RackParents that is designed to support working parents. We created an opportunity for them to connect with the neighborhood by volunteering at the local YMCA branch, which is down the road from Rackspace, by hosting a kids' trunk-or-treat event in the parking lot. The event was meaningful to members of RackParents because they were passionate about doing work that was focused on kids and families. The event also helped serve our neighborhood's kids.

- **Use internal and external branding.** Branding can be accomplished in many ways, and it's important to include because it makes this type of work part of your company's ethos. Showcasing your logo on signage during a community-based activity is certainly helpful, but you can also create specially designed volunteer or donor T-shirts to help with both internal and external branding recognition. Don't have the budget for a shirt? Perhaps arrange to have employees all wear the same color, their name tags, or any other item that shows solidarity. Larger companies often have clever names for their give-back programs, but there's nothing stopping even the smallest startup from creating an internal name and brand around such work. Doing so suddenly amplifies the focus and makes what might at first seem like a value-add activity become more official.

- **Communicate consciously.** Think about all the places and ways your employees receive communications. Formally, there are meetings, newsletters, email, bulletin boards, intranets, social media, and myriad other channels. Informally, your employees look at, listen to, and share information in countless other places. In a "noisy" environment, it's important to cut through that noise to get the word out—both about what your company has already accomplished in the community and which opportunities are coming up. It's also important for those outside your organization to hear about what you're doing. Create consistency in the timing and format of your formal communications—both internal and external—and allow influencers inside and outside the organization to help carry your messages.

- **Don't force it.** No one likes to be "voluntold" to get involved. Personally, I'm not a fan of mandated community involvement, especially when the expectation is that you have to volunteer or donate in order to be considered for leadership roles. As a business leader, create the opportunity to get involved, support those who participate, and release the rest.

- **Don't forget the fun.** Rackspace's annual Thanksgiving food drive has always been centered on donating food during the holidays, and in its early years, one of the Rackspace sales teams put its own spin on making the donation. Rather than individuals simply making monetary contributions, the team pooled donations and went to the nearby grocery store with a list of the foods needed. Team members raced around the store to see who could find the items first, similar to the *Supermarket Sweep* game show. Donating $20 to feed a hungry family never felt so fun! Instead of individually filling boxes with the requisite canned goods and food staples, they turned the activity into a fun (and public!) team competition. As a bonus, that day other shoppers in the grocery store were exposed to Rackspace and how excited Rackers get about volunteer projects. Remember that fun goes a long way in any program's success, and there's no better time for fun than when getting involved in the community.

- **Bring (friendly) competition into the mix.** When it comes to giving back, a little competition never hurt anybody. Consider a competition between business unit leaders or creating an exclusive event for those who raise the most funds or volunteer the most hours. Several years ago, the Rackspace Foundation re-created a high school prom exclusive to our donors. The only way to attend was to already be or become a donor, and we had prizes for attendees who brought in the most donors. It sounds silly, but the prom was a real hit with employees. It doesn't have to be that complex, though; it could be as simple as winning bragging rights among the other teams. For your purposes, cast a wide net to figure out what drives your employees.

- **Be inclusive.** In corporate philanthropy, there's often a substantial distinction between the people who experience the perceived perks of this work and everybody else. Often, events are exclusive to executives or those who directly manage the programs. I would encourage you to ignore that old way of operating and open those opportunities up to all employees. Create committees to help you make grant-making decisions. Rotate who gets access to exclusive events. Share decision-making and leadership when choosing where to focus your community efforts. Create a culture of inclusiveness in this work.

- **Involve executives.** One of the best ways to make community investment programs stick is to have executives participate in and champion different programs. Doing so creates opportunities for frontline employees to work side by side with the leaders they follow. It also shows that leaders walk the talk and that giving back isn't just paying lip service. When a business leader takes time out of their busy schedule to volunteer or makes a donation to a cause, it sends a message of integrity and puts the leader on equal footing with employees. It also creates a new lens through which employees see their leaders.

GOOD FOR BUSINESS

Data shows that in today's employment marketplace, people—and millennials and Gen Z in particular—increasingly choose to work for companies that demonstrate commitment to the world and the communities around them. So even though the Rackspace Foundation's enrichment programs are good for the community, they are also good for Rackspace. They attract a rich talent pool and demonstrate the company's values in a tangible way.

Beyond simply attracting talent, social investment programs also *retain* talent. Across all of Rackspace's engagement surveys—which, as you'll recall, rate Rackspace employees at more than double the national average for this sentiment—the highest-ranking indicator to satisfaction during my tenure there was that employees "feel proud of contributions Rackspace makes in the community."

Soon enough, that engagement governs productivity and begins to snowball. Talent attraction becomes easier, brand recognition goes up, and the company gains positive publicity. The community trusts and admires the organization, and stakeholders feel connected to the company and brand.

Although this story focuses on the Rackspace Foundation and the impacts it has had on Rackspace, our experience is by no means an outlier. This book is your company's call to action and can become your story, too.

WHAT'S NEXT?

At the end of the day, your goal is to help people, and no matter what your company does—whether you make sandwiches or deliver packages—there's a way you can tie your work to a local need. While you benefit your customers, you also have an opportunity to benefit your employees, the communities around you, and the organization as a whole.

Now that you've identified the power of building employee engagement into your program, pull out the playbook you brainstormed in Chapter 3. How can you optimize your strategy? Who are you going to call first? As we wrap up our time together, look for ways to keep the momentum going. You've got communities to help.

CONCLUSION

We met Quentin when he was in seventh grade at one of the Rackspace Foundation's adopted schools. Unbeknownst to us, he made a promise to himself early on that he wouldn't be brought down by his surroundings, and he vowed to go to college. That year, he was paired with a Racker, Grant, in our mentoring program who stayed with him through middle and high school.

Because he took part in the mentoring program and stayed connected to Grant, Quentin realized he could pursue a degree in IT. His first big win was graduating from high school. His second big win was attending Texas State University in San Marcos, about an hour away from San Antonio. By the time you're reading this, Quentin will have graduated and become gainfully employed. Over the years, we saw Quentin get asked to give a keynote speech about the impact of his mentoring experience to an audience that included city leaders, business leaders, and politicians, including then-mayor of San Antonio Julian Castro. While Grant stood beside him through the ups and downs over the years, it was Quentin who saw a different future for himself. It was Quentin who stuck with the program and saw how it could be a lever for him. "For me, Rackspace meant a future," Quentin says. "While I'd always been adept at computing and enjoyed learning about programming, lunches at Rackspace and meeting people who were in a field I wanted to be in made it that much more tangible. The memories of it and where I wanted to be are part of what keep me going when I STRUGGLED in college. Grant's lessons about life and the field stick with me to this day."

Grant's experience of mentoring Quentin is also notable. "As I've seen Quentin grow through the years, I have always been impressed by how well he is able to avoid distractions and stay the course. He has always known what he's wanted to pursue and works hard to realize his plans even when he's encountered setbacks. I've always been impressed by his grit and determination, and today, I am even more impressed by the man he has become," Grant says.

Then, there's Mercedes. She had a very chaotic home life. Her mother struggled with substance abuse, and Mercedes was responsible for looking after and raising her half-siblings. If you'll remember, Rackspace is right beside a major highway that divides part of the area of adopted schools, and when Mercedes was in high school, she was one of the kids who had to walk across IH-35 every day to get to school. She made a way to get to school because she knew it was her way out.

Initially, Mercedes had no idea what Rackspace was; she just knew it was a big company next door to her high school. Then, when she started looking for an internship her senior year, she knocked on Rackspace's door. She ended up impressing everybody at the company by interning as an event planner. Her boss, Jaime, took her under her wing and showed her not only the ins and outs of working at a "real job" but also navigating life as a young adult. She saw how she could create a different future for herself. "I like to think of my time at Rackspace as being born again," Mercedes says. "This is a place that helped me grow from the moment I stepped in the door. I was only sixteen, and Rackspace gave me so many mentors. People that were my peers, but connected with me on a level of understanding that I hadn't received before."

Mercedes's connection goes deeper than just mentorship. "When people ask me why I love Rackspace so much, and it's because they've always treated me like family, and they *were* my family when I had nowhere else to turn. It's in the culture of who we are as Rackers. Which is not something that you often find in people. I love my Rackspace family. I will forever be grateful for having such an amazing support system of people who've watched me grow so much in these past years. So, yes, Rackspace is everything to my life."

Mercedes went on to attend Texas Lutheran University and get her degree in social entrepreneurship with a minor in communications. Because of her drive and the fact that Rackers believed in her and got her thinking about the different paths available in her life, Mercedes was able to escape the cycle of generational poverty and drug addiction. Connections she made through Rackspace changed her life. In Jaime's words, "Mentoring isn't always easy. Mercedes and I had our rough times. But I believe that it's worth it. Mercedes had a place in my heart and on my team where she *belonged*. I always want her to know that she is loved and that lots of people are invested in her because they see her potential."

I like to think of Quentin and Mercedes as the poster children of the Rackspace Foundation's mission. They have done so well in their young lives and owned their trajectory, which, one could argue, began when one company reached out to their neighbors and asked how they could help. When I hear these kids speak about the impact of the foundation, I realize how much this work matters. We're really doing something special in the community—and you could be doing the same in yours.

START TODAY

My goal for this book isn't to start a conversation about what Rackspace does in its neighborhood; my goal is to start a conversation about what *your* company can do in *your* neighborhood.

If you've read this far, I'm talking to you. If you've picked up this book and stayed the course, you are the person for the job. This is a pep talk I give myself all the time. If you're curious enough to notice there are challenges that need to be addressed and can think of potential solutions, you're in the right place. Make now the right time.

As you dip your toe in the water, think about your business as an asset. A lot of businesses feel like they don't belong in the education realm philanthropically because they don't know how schools operate. Guess what? Most schools feel the same way. At the end of the day, though, everyone is learning new roles and ways of working. We are learning about one another as we go.

Look at your business from an asset perspective and consider what you can bring to the table. Money is a big component, but you can contribute more than money. Maybe you can contribute time, talent, or employees. Maybe you can encourage new ways of thinking. Maybe you could be a point of contact for schools to call. Even if you can't say yes to every request, offering an email address or a phone number could make a huge difference. That way, you're telling schools that they are not alone.

In doing so, you'll need to buck the mentality that you only want to support the winners. I get it; most well-intentioned companies will seek out kids with high potential who are likely already on a path to college and support them. There is less risk involved in this approach. If you support a student who is going to college anyway, you're assured of success.

The mentality is different when supporting students through enrichment programs. By implementing these initiatives, you're creating access for *all* students. You're leveling the playing field. You're normalizing positive childhood experiences for children. You're helping, in your own way, to create more equity for them.

Whether your kids actually come out on top is inconsequential. "Top" is relative anyway. You aren't making any less of an investment as long as you are helping kids access opportunities.

THE "NO" NARRATIVE ENDS WITH YOU

Your mission is to support everyone you can reach. This goes beyond the high-potential kids who are already achieving high marks. If your goal is to help a community, you can't create community transformation for some and not others. Instead, you need to figure out how to create equal opportunity for anybody to take advantage of.

As you move forward, you'll likely find that you aren't alone in wanting to give back. People will want to opt in, and for community transformation to happen, you'll need them to. Approach these interactions with an open mind and a listening ear. Be willing to learn. Be willing to give. Be willing to end the narrative for kids in these communities that have historically denied them opportunities. Instead of reminding these kids of what they don't have, show them what they do—then add to it.

Yes, you will face critics. Some may even be in your office. However, as Theodore Roosevelt once said:

> It is not the critic who counts, not the man who points out how the strong man stumbles, or where the doer of deeds could have done them better. The credit belongs to the man who is actually in the arena, whose face is marred by dust and sweat and blood; who strives valiantly; who

errs, who comes short again and again, because there is no effort without error and shortcoming; but who does actually strive to do the deeds; who knows great enthusiasms, the great devotions; who spends himself in a worthy cause; who at the best knows in the end the triumph of high achievement, and who at the worst, if he fails, at least fails while daring greatly, so that his place shall never be with those cold and timid souls who neither know victory nor defeat.

Don't be the critic. Be the helper.

GO, GO, GO!

There is real potential for a movement in which corporations and schools come closer together in partnership. This movement can create incredible outcomes. Even if you help one student, that's a win.

Your next move? Make that phone call. Send that email. Stop by that location and introduce yourself. Stop aiming for perfection because it doesn't exist. The time will never be perfect, and neither will you. Even as I write this, I know there are ways the Rackspace Foundation can improve and be of more service to our communities; we're getting there. In the meantime, though, we are showing up for our kids every day, and they see us. More importantly, they know that we see them. And that they matter.

Use the advice in this book and run with it. I encourage you to make it your own.

After all, the next generation is watching. Together, we can give them the boost they need for a better collective future.

ACKNOWLEDGMENTS

I would like to start by saying that many years ago, before I even started working at Rackspace, much less in the capacity of the foundation, I had a dream of doing transformational, place-based work—before I even knew that "place-based" was a thing. At the time, I was a regular volunteer at Wheatley Courts, a San Antonio Housing Authority complex that later became a US Department of Education Promise Neighborhoods. I hoped—prayed—that I would someday have a "real" role doing the work I felt compelled to do at Wheatley. But it was just little old me with a regular job and a tiny dream, and I didn't know how that would ever come to fruition. But I held on to it and, in doing so, stepped into my future. So I'd like to first acknowledge that sense of purpose that was placed on my heart. It was the thing I couldn't let go of. I'm honored that it chose me.

Doing this work is by no means a solo act. There are so many people who enabled, encouraged, and made room for the work in Rackspace's adopted schools. I owe a debt of gratitude to all the individuals, partners, and organizations I had the great fortune of working with along the way.

At North East ISD's Central Office—in particular, Dr. Brian Gottardy, Colleen Bohrmann, Eric Wicker, Amy Lane, Dr. Alicia Thomas, Dr. Richard Middleton, and Ron Clary. Thank you for your trust and for joining us on this journey. We created something really special.

At the seven schools—the leadership teams and administrators, the teachers, family specialists, counselors, those who put up their hands to volunteer their time and energy, the thought partners, the idea kick-arounders, the collaborators, and especially the ones who poured into our kids each day. You are the heroes. Thank you.

Our nonprofit partners—Communities in Schools of San Antonio, Youth Orchestras of San Antonio, SAY Sí, Gemini Ink, Girlstart, Good Samaritan Community Services, College Advising Corps, our chess coaches Alex Weinberg and Rheanna English, Youth Code Jam, Trinity University College Advising Corps, and others who were part of the foundation portfolio over the years. Thank you for doing the work you do and for learning with us along the way.

The people and organizations we entrusted with the desire to learn more and become better—Westat, for helping us understand the power of logic models and unified metrics; Christine Drennon, PhD, with Trinity University's Department of Urban Studies, who helped us see our neighborhood in its completeness and helped give better directionality to our passion; and Dr. Drennon's Urban Studies students, who worked alongside us doing the research.

I want to acknowledge the Rackspace Foundation board members past and present, many of whom also filled the role of advocate, trusted advisor, and friend: Anna Ziegler, Kathy Kersten, Mari Aguirre, Alan Schoenbaum, Graham Weston, Karl Pichler, Jason Hopkins, Lisa McLin, Holly Windham, Louis Alterman, Rachel Woodson, Patty Freeman, Jason Bowling, Matt Stoyka, Summer Gafford, and Stephanie Box. Thank you for backing this work and guiding its growth. Thank you for supporting me in this work.

My team over the years—Molly Salmon, Annie Vu, Allie Patterson, Cristina Ruiz-Goodwin, Daniel Sherrill, Ashley Metke, and Amanda Cowan. I'm not sure I can put into words how much you all have meant to me. Thank you for being all-in for our kids. Thank you for making me a better leader. Thank you for your friendship. I am so incredibly grateful for each of you.

There are several people who don't belong in any particular category but were nonetheless instrumental in making this book and/or this work happen. Whether you were a thought partner, a co-conspirator, an advocate, a confidante, a source of wisdom or motivation, thank you: Lanham Napier, Pat Condon, Dirk Elmendorf, Lew Moorman, Dan Goodgame, Brett Elmendorf, Judy McCarter, Rebecca Sterling, Ellen Coomber, Jessica Weaver, John Hinds, Melvin Echard, Bethany Lorge, Tamara Hudgins, and Kayla Rice. My Creative Council sisterhood: Tracy Loring, Carrie Nuyalis, Suzette Conway, and Moriah Olearnek Rappold. The incredible team at Scribe who were infinitely patient and insightful, beginning with Jessica Burdg (so many thanks to you!), Libby Allen, Kayla Sokol, and JT McCormick. My fellow travelers on this literary road: Lorenzo Gomez and Carlos Maestas. And to my friends and family who showed me so much encouragement not only throughout the process of creating this book but throughout the long journey of figuring this work out.

To all the Rackers: thank you. You cared deeply about this work. You put your money behind this work. When I left Rackspace, our average per-paycheck donation to the Rackspace Foundation was $16.36. Over time, we gave more than $5 million to programs in our adopted schools. Look what an impact you had on future generations simply by saying yes. As Lanham used to say, "Rackers are a special breed of people," and it remains true.

Last but perhaps most importantly, Graham Weston. Graham, you have an incredible way of making things happen. Things that don't always necessarily follow the "normal" path and definitely things that, at first pass, seem impossible. What you did for

Rackspace, for Rackers, and for our community simply cannot be captured with words. Thank you for believing in me. You changed the course of my path in more ways than I can count, and you will always be a hero to me.

Rackspace today may look and feel very different than the Rackspace described in this book, but one thing that we can all say is that we created something special together. The Rackspace Foundation was just one of countless aspects of a very special company that, as Lanham also used to say, sought to make a dent in the universe. And we did.

—C

ABOUT THE AUTHOR

CARA NICHOLS spent ten years helping San Antonio's biggest and most important technology company redefine corporate philanthropy and community engagement. Perhaps what influenced her approach most was her early-on experience as an elementary school teacher both in the district where Rackspace resides and also in a rural district without access to critical programs and services. In that setting, she saw kids struggling with poverty and other adult-sized problems every day, yet she often felt powerless to help them. Through her work with the Rackspace Foundation, Cara brought different stakeholders together—businesses, nonprofits, and schools—to address many of the challenges facing their community and ultimately helped create a new model of corporate philanthropy. Today, Cara consults with companies and foundations to help them invest in their communities in more impactful, authentic ways. Find out more at www.threefolded.com.

CPSIA information can be obtained
at www.ICGtesting.com
Printed in the USA
LVHW111120080522
717899LV00001B/4